Recipes

from the

Grave

Recipes

from the

Grave

Wonderful Dishes for the

Here and After

P. Arden Corbin

Recipes from the Grave

ISBN-13: 978-1516931286
ISBN-10: 1516931289

V 8.26.15

Contents

PART ONE

In this part, there are Recipes whereby all of the contributors are deceased. Not from eating their own recipes, but from natural causes like old age or from some kind of terminal disease they caught while living their lives on this Earth.

Some of these recipes are most probably as old as a hundred years, and were baked or cooked on stoves that were fueled by using wood or coal or corn cobs or Cow chips or maybe even Buffalo chips that were found on some of the various prairies of some of our plains states.

Considering how some of these recipes were created, please try all of them, because you will find that they are all very well crafted.

Teresa Philadelphia Corbin Henderson

ABBREVIATIONS

ctn.	carton
gal.	gallon
lb.	pound
oz.	ounce
pkg.	package
qt.	quart
Tbsp.	tablespoon
teasp.	teaspoon
tsp.	teaspoon
sq.	square
sqrs.	squares
pkgs.	packages
T.	Tablespoon

ALL
RECIPES
ARE IN
ALPHABETICAL
ORDER

* * *

ALMONDS CRESCENTS

Linda Kirk Pierce—Deceased

1 lb. butter
4 level cups flour
1½ cups powdered sugar
½ lb. ground almonds

Combine and mix all ingredients. Shape with hands into crescent shapes and lay out on a cookie sheet.

Bake at 350 degrees until lightly brown.

Partly cool then roll in powdered sugar.

*   *   *

ALMOND ROCA

Jean Bruinier Nash—Deceased

1-cup sugar
½ lb. butter
½ lb. blanched almonds
¼ cup water
1 Tbsp. Karo syrup
½ lb. Hershey chocolate bars

Put first five ingredients into a heavy pan, cook to hard crack stage, or until almonds are toasted light brown, stirring constantly. Pour into pan to cool and spread with melted chocolate while candy is still hot.

Cool and break into pieces.

* * *

ANN LANDERS MEAT LOAF

Ann Landers—Deceased

2 lbs. ground round steak
2 eggs
1½ cups bread crumbs
¾ cup ketchup
1 tsp. accent
½ cup warm water
1 pkg. Lipton's onion soup mix
2 strips bacon
1 can (8 oz.) tomato sauce

Combine all but bacon and tomato sauce. Put into loaf pan. Cover with two strips of bacon if you like flavor. Pour tomato sauce over all.

Bake one hour at 350 degrees. Serves six.

* * *

APPLE SAUCE CAKE

Neva Martin Hazen Ruth—Deceased

$1/3$ to ½ cup shortening
½ tsp. salt
Rounded tsp. cinnamon and cloves
1-cup sugar
1 egg, unbeaten
1-cup applesauce
¾ cup chopped nuts
1¼ cup flour
1 tsp. soda

Cream shortening and sugar and add remaining ingredients and mix well. Bake at 350 degrees for 40 minutes.

* * *

APPLE SAUCE FRUIT CAKE

Alma Fehrs Corbin—Deceased

½ cup butter
1 cup sugar
1½ cup sweetened applesauce
3 cups flour
2 tsp. soda
½ tsp. salt
½ tsp cinnamon
½ tsp. cloves
½ tsp. nutmeg
½ cup citron
1½ cup dates, 1 cup raisins, 1½ cup nuts

Cream butter and sugar. Add applesauce and blend thoroughly. Add 2 cups flour, sifted, with soda, salt, and spices. Stir only to blend well. Mix remaining cup of flour with chopped fruit and nuts. Stir into batter. (Other mixed glazed fruits may be added to make a real fruit cake).

Pour into two 5 x 9 inch loaf pans. Bake in a slow oven (300 degrees) one hour. Store in tightly covered containers.

* * *

APPLE SAUCE FRUIT CAKE

Lulu Corbin Nash—Deceased

1-cup butter
2 cups brown sugar
½ cup dark syrup
½ cup molasses
2 cups unsweetened applesauce
2 tsp. soda in sauce
1 tsp. each of cinnamon, cloves and nutmeg
3 eggs well beaten

Mix in ½ cup of fruit, raisins, currants, dates, nuts, and gum drops. Add to mixture about 4-½ cups flour. Pour into a pan of desired size. Bake at 300 degrees for 1 to 2 hours, depending on the size of the pan. Let it set for two hours right side up after removing it from Oven. Then run knife all the way around pan to separate cake from pan. Then turn upside down with four salad forks placed between cake and pan on all four sides and let cake fall to counter top on wax paper. When on wax paper, wrap in same and place in refrigerator on lower shelf for safekeeping.

* * *

BAKED PINEAPPLE GINGER APPLES

Peggy Chapman Corbin—Deceased

8 oz. can juice-packed crushed pineapples
½ tsp. ground ginger
6 baking apples, cored

Drain pineapple well, reserving the juice. Stir ginger into pineapple. Spoon pineapple into cored apples. Stand apples in a non-stick baking dish just large enough to hold them and pour on reserved pineapple juice. Bake uncovered about 20 to 25 minutes in a preheated 350-degree oven, basting often with pan juices. Serves six.

* * *

BANANA NUT BREAD

Olive Brice Grace—Deceased

I received this recipe in 1947 from my aunt in Madison, Wisconsin

½ cup butter
2 cups flour
1 cup sugar
1 tsp, soda
2 eggs
½ tsp. salt
2 bananas
½ cup nutmeats

Crush bananas and whip until very light. Cream butter and sugar, and eggs, then flour, soda, salt, and nut meats. Add bananas, turn into well-greased bread pan.

Bake in cold {not preheated} oven for 1 hour at 350 degrees.

* * *

BAR-B-Q SMOKIES

Linda Kirk Pierce—Deceased

1 jar grape jelly
2 or 3 pkgs. Little smokies
4 Tbsp. mustard {add more to taste}

Place grape jelly in crock-pot on high setting, stirring occasionally. When liquefied, stir in mustard, mixing well. When sauce is desired consistency and taste, remove from heat and add the smokies.

Serve as appetizers on toothpicks.

* * *

BEEF CASSEROLE

Delores Storly Corbin—Deceased

2 lbs. ground beef
1 onion, cut up
Crumbs from a 1 lb. loaf of bread
1 tsp. poultry seasoning
1 can of celery soup
2 cans cream of chicken soup
¼ cup butter

Put raw ground beef in large cake pan. Put cut-up onion on top of beef. Spread breadcrumbs over onions and press down in ground beef. Combine poultry seasoning, celery soup, cream of chicken soup and butter. Heat soup mixture to boiling. Pour over meat and bread mixture. Bake 1 hour at 350 degrees

* * *

BEAN CASSEROLE

Neva Martin Hazen Ruth—Deceased

2-Tbsp. butter
1 lb. ground beef
1 pkg. onion soup mix
½ cup water
1 cup catsup
2 tsp. vinegar
2 1-lb. cans pork and beans in tomato sauce
1 1-lb. cans kidney beans, drained
2 Tbsp. prepared mustard

Brown beef in butter. Stir in remaining ingredients and pour into bean pot or casserole. Bake at 400 degrees for 30 minutes.

* * *

BEANIE HOT DISH

Roger Pitzl—Deceased

Brown 1 lb. hamburger with chopped onion, drain. Add 1 can pork and beans and 1 can French-cut green beans, drained. Stir and heat thoroughly. You can put dollops of mashed potatoes on top, if you like.

*   *   *

BEEF FILLETS WITH MUSHROOM SAUCE

Margaret {Peggy} Ann Corbin—Deceased

2 lbs. beef fillets
½ cup butter
1 small clove garlic, mashed
3 Tbsp. Brandy
Salt and Pepper
2 shallots, minced
1 pt. mushrooms, drained
½ cup whipping cream

Cut meat into ¾ inch thick medallions. Pound to flatten slightly. Sprinkle lightly with salt and pepper. Melt 2-Tbsp. butter in skillet. Add meat and sauté over high heat, turning once. Reduce heat and cook 5 to 6 minutes longer or until done. Set aside. Melt 2-Tbsp. butter in skillet. Add shallots and garlic. Sauté until tender. Add mushrooms and sauté 2 minutes. Add brandy and reduce to glaze.

Stir in whipping cream. Stir in remaining ¼ cup butter until melted.

Correct seasoning. Serve with meat. Serves six easily.

* * *

BLEU CHEESE DRESSING

Olive Brice Grace— Deceased

MIX TOGETHER:
1 pint mayonnaise
½ cup buttermilk
3 oz. bleu cheese, flaked
½ cup evaporated milk

* * *

BLUEBERRY MUFFINS

Alma Fehrs Corbin—Deceased

1 cup blueberries, frozen
2 eggs
¾ cup sugar
5 Tbsp. melted butter
1 cup milk
½ tsp. salt
2½ cup flour, sifted

Shake frozen blueberries up in ½ cup of the flour. Resift flour with baking powder, salt, and sugar. Beat eggs add to the milk. Add this to dry ingredients and then the berries. Just before putting in the oven, add the melted butter. Put in greased muffin tins and bake in a 400-degree oven for about 15 minutes. Yields 18 to 24 muffins.

*   *   *

BOILED SEVEN-MINUTE ICING

Linda Kirk Pierce—Deceased

1 egg white, unbeaten
3 Tbsp. cold water
7/8 cup granulated sugar
½ tsp. vanilla flavored extract

Place all ingredients in the top of a double boiler.

Place over boiling water and beat with a rotary beater for 7 minutes. Remove from heat and beat one minute more. Spread.

For chocolate icing:

Add to above 1½ oz. unsweetened chocolate two minutes before removing from heat.

For coffee taste:

use cold boiled coffee in place of cold water.

* * *

BOILED RAISIN COOKIES

Lulu Corbin Nash—Deceased

Place 1 cup raisins in 1 cup of boiling water for fifteen minutes then let cool.

Cream together: 2 cups sugar, 1 cup shortening, and 3 eggs.

Add cooled raisins and mix well
Add:
4 cups flour
1½ tsp. cinnamon
1 tsp. baking powder
¼ tsp. nutmeg
1 tsp. soda
¼ tsp. cloves
1 tsp. salt

Mix all of the ingredients well in mixing bowl. When mixture has the desired consistency of cookie dough then place dough on floured Cheesecloth, roll out with rolling pin until 1/8-inch thickness, then cut out cookies of desired sizes and shapes. Place on cookie sheet and bake at temperature noted below.

Bake at 375 degrees until done.

* * *

BRAUNSCHWEIGER DIP

Linda Kirk Pierce—Deceased

8 oz. Braunschweiger
8 oz. cream cheese
1 Tbsp. Worcestershire sauce
1 Tbsp. diced onions

Combine ingredients with an electric mixer, chill.
Serve with chips or crackers.

* * *

BROWN SUGAR FUDGE

Linda Kirk Pierce—Deceased

3 cups brown sugar
1¼ cups milk
9 Tbsp. white corn syrup

Combine ingredients, place over high heat, stirring constantly, just to boiling. Reduce heat to medium low, cook 30 minutes more. Test to a soft boil.

Then add:
½ cup peanut butter
1 tsp. vanilla
2 tsp. butter

Let cool for five minutes. Then beat for five minutes, then put in a buttered pan and let set for about an hour.

* * *

BURNT SUGAR ANGEL FOOD CAKE

Alma Fehrs Corbin—Deceased

1½ cups cake flour, un-sifted
1½ tsp. cream of tartar
2 cups sugar
2 Tbsp. burnt sugar syrup
1½ cups egg whites from 10 to 12 eggs
1tsp. vanilla flavoring
$1/3$ cup chopped pecans
¼ tsp. salt

Sift flour 6 times. Measure 1½ cups. Add sugar. Sift 2 times. Add salt to egg whites. Beat until stiff but not dry. Add cream of tartar. Beat until egg whites stand in peaks. Carefully fold flour-sugar mixture into egg whites. Gradually add burnt sugar syrup and vanilla flavoring. Blend carefully. Sprinkle bottom of un-oiled tube pan with nuts. Pour batter over nuts. Bake in slow oven (325 degrees) for 1 hour.

Invert pan on rack. Let cake hang until cool. To make burnt sugar syrup, place ½ cup sugar in a small pan. Place over medium heat. Stir constantly until golden brown.

Add ¼ cup boiling water, stirring constantly until sugar is melted.

Cool. Store in a Jar.

* * *

BUTTER FUDGE FINGERS

Olive Brice Grace—Deceased

2 squares unsweetened chocolate (2-oz)
1/3 cup butter
1 cup sugar
2 eggs
½ tsp. baking powder
¾ cup flour
½ cup nutmeats
½ tsp. salt

Heat oven to 350 degrees. Melt chocolate and butter over hot water. Beat in sugar and eggs. Sift dry ingredients together, stir into liquid mixture. Add nuts. Spread in greased 8-inch square pan. Bake for 30—35 minutes, until top has dull crust. Do not overbake. Cool slightly. Make topping. Spread on brownies. When set, cut in 2 x 1-inch fingers. Makes about 32.

To make the topping: Brown ¼ cup soft butter over medium heat. Blend with 2 cups sifted confectioner's sugar. Blend in 2 Tbsp. cream and 1 tsp. vanilla. Spread on brownies. Melt 1 square of unsweetened chocolate (1 oz.) and 1 Tbsp.

* * *

BUTTERSCOTCH BARS

Lulu Corbin Nash—Deceased

½ cup coconut
2 eggs
1 cup sugar
½ cup nuts
2 cups marshmallows, small
¾ cup butter
2½ cups crushed graham crackers
2 tsp. peanut butter
1 pkg. butterscotch chips

Beat eggs add sugar and butter. Boil slowly for 2 minutes. Cool slightly. Add graham crackers, coconut, nuts, and marshmallows.

Press in 9 x 13 inch pan. Top with package of butterscotch chips melted with 3 tsp. peanut butter.

* * *

CAKE DOUGHNUTS

Ruth Corbin Graves—Deceased

4½ cups flour, sifted
3 eggs
¼ tsp. nutmeg
1 cup sugar
¼ tsp. allspice
3 Tbsp. shortening, melted
1 cup buttermilk or sour milk
1½ tsp. soda
1½ tsp. cream of tartar
1½ tsp. salt
Fat for deep-frying

Sift together flour, nutmeg, allspice, soda, cream of tartar and salt. Beat eggs until thick and creamy and lemon colored, and then gradually beat in the sugar. Add the melted shortening and buttermilk, and then add the flour mixture. Mix well, chill, and turn out on floured board or pastry cloth. Roll to ¼ inch thick, cut with floured cutter. Fry a few at a time in deep hot fat at 375 degrees for 3 minutes or until brown, first on one side and then on the other.

(Backstory)

This cake doughnut recipe is similar to one used by Alma Fehrs Corbin, during the depression years of the 1930's and early 1940's. She always made several batches of these during the harvest season when the threshing rig would set up on the Corbin farm to thresh the bundles of grain. It was necessary to take "lunch" to the hands mid-morning and mid-afternoon. So the cake doughnuts and coffee were taken out to the field in the morning. These doughnuts were deep fried in lard, and Dad (Clarence Corbin) usually ate more than his share and wound up with a bellyache.

When we were about 16 to 18 years old, sister Peggy and I would usually take the lunches out to the threshing crew, and spike pitch (help throw bundles off the hay rack wagons into the thresher feeder with 3 tined forks) while the men ate their lunch. That way no threshing time was lost. Coffee was made in a large pot with pouring spout handle, with coffee placed directly in the water and boiled. It was necessary to add beaten egg whites to settle the coffee grounds to the bottom of the pot.

* * *

CARAMEL LICK BARS

Linda Kirk Pierce—Deceased

1 pkg. Pillsbury white cake mix
1 cup chopped nuts
½ cup solid shortening
2 eggs
1 cup caramel ice cream topping
2 tsp. hot water

Combine all ingredients, beat three minutes. Spread batter in a jelly roll pan. Bake for 25 to 30 minutes at 325 degrees.

The bar will be soft with high ridges and flat center.

Cool completely. Spread frosting. Let stand for one hour before cutting into bars.

To make Frosting, use:
    2 cups powdered sugar
    2 Tbsp. milk
    $1/3$ cup butter, softened
    3 Tbsp. caramel topping

Combine ingredients and beat well

*   *   *

CARAMEL ROLLS

Linda Kirk Pierce—Deceased

$2/3$ cup thick cream {whipping cream}
$2/3$ cup brown sugar
1 loaf frozen bread dough, thawed
¾ cup white sugar
Add Cinnamon to taste

Combine cream and brown sugar in a 9 by 13 inch pan, place on heat and bring to a slow boil, sprinkle with cinnamon, then let cool. Roll out dough on a floured board. Spread with butter. Sprinkle with cinnamon and white sugar. Roll up and cut into 1 inch slices. Place rolls in caramel and let rise to double their normal size. Bake at 350 degrees for 20 to 30 minutes. Remove from oven and tip over onto cookie sheet. Lined with four layers of wax paper, letting caramel drip over rolls.

* * *

CHEESE BALL

Linda Kirk Pierce—Deceased

2 8-oz.pkgs. Philadelphia Cream Cheese
2 8-oz.pkgs. Cracker Barrel Cheese, grated
1 pkg. Braunschweiger
1 tsp. lemon juice
1 Tbsp. pimento
1 Tbsp. chopped pepper
1 Tbsp. chopped onion
2 Tbsp. Worcestershire sauce

Mix together all ingredients. Form into ball or log.
Chill for four hours. Roll in Parsley flakes. Serve with crackers

* * *

CHICKEN BREASTS DIANE

Peggy Chapman Corbin—Deceased

4 large boneless chicken breasts halved or 8 small ones
2 Tbsp. butter or margarine
3 Tbsp. chopped fresh chives or green onions
2 tsp. Dijon style mustard
2 Tbsp. Brandy or cognac, optional
½ tsp. salt
¼ to ½ tsp. black pepper
A Tbsp. of chopped parsley
¼ cup chicken broth
Juice of ½ lemon or lime

Place chicken breasts halves between sheets of waxed paper or plastic wrap. Pound slightly with Mallet. Sprinkle with salt and black pepper. Heat 1 Tbsp. each of oil and butter in large skillet. Cook chicken over high heat for 2 minutes on each side. Do not cook longer or they will be overcooked and dry. Transfer to warm serving platter. Add chives or green onion, lime juice, brandy, parsley, and mustard to pan. Cook 15 seconds, whisking constantly. Whisk into broth. Stir until sauce is smooth. Whisk in remaining butter and oil. Pour sauce over chicken.

Serve immediately. Makes 4 servings easily.

* * *

CHICKEN MIX

Jean Bruinier Nash—Deceased

1 4-lb. chicken or 4 medium fryers, cut up
½ tsp. pepper
4 carrots, peeled, chopped
4 qt. cold water
4 tsp. salt
3 Tbsp. parsley flakes
2 tsp. basil

Combine all ingredients in a large kettle or Dutch oven. Cover and cook over high heat until water boils. Simmer until meat is tender, about 1-½ hours. Remove from heat. Strain broth and refrigerate until fat can be skimmed. Cool chicken, then remove and discard bones and skin. Put chicken into six 1-pint freezer containers, leaving ½ inch space at top. Pour skimmed chicken broth into six more 1 pint containers, with ½ inch space at top.

Seal and label containers.

Use within three months. Makes about 6 pints of chicken mix and about 6 pints of chicken broth.

* * *

CHOCOLATE CHIP COOKIES

Ruth Corbin Graves—Deceased

1 cup butter or margarine
¾ cup sugar
¾ cup light brown sugar
1 tsp. vanilla
1 cup chopped nuts (optional)
2¼ cups flour
1 tsp. baking soda
½ tsp. salt
1 11 oz. pkg, milk chocolate chips
2 eggs

Cream butter, sugar, brown sugar, and vanilla until light and fluffy. Add eggs, beat well. Combine flour and baking soda and add to mixture, gradually beat until a creamy mixture. Stir in nuts and chips. Drop by teaspoonful onto ungreased cookie sheet. Bake at 375 degrees for 8 to 10 minutes or until lightly browned. Cool slightly and remove from cookie sheet.

Makes about 6 dozen cookies.

* * *

CHOCOLATE SUNDAE BROWNIES

Delores Storly Corbin—Deceased

¼ cup soft margarine
1 cup sugar
1 1-lb can chocolate syrup
4 eggs
1 cup plus 1 Tbsp. flour
½ tsp. baking powder
½ cup chopped walnuts (optional)
1 tsp. vanilla

Mix ingredients in this order: Margarine, sugar, eggs, syrup, flour, baking powder, walnuts and vanilla.

Spread in large pan (10 x 15 inches) Bake 30 minutes. Spread on frosting.

Frosting:
   6 Tbsp. milk
   6 Tbsp. margarine
   1⅓ cups sugar

Bring to boil and boil only 30 seconds. Remove from heat, add ½ cup chocolate chips. Beat until smooth, add 1 tsp. vanilla.

Spread on frosting while the baked mixture is still quite warm.

Frosting will firm almost as soon as it is spread.

* * *

CHOCOLATE SYRUP BROWNIES

Peggy Ann Corbin—Deceased

¾ cup chocolate flavored syrup, canned
½ cup butter
1 cup all-purpose flour
1 cup sugar
2 tsp. vanilla extract
3 eggs
¾ cup chopped walnuts or pecans
Dash of salt
Pecans or walnuts, for garnish

In a bowl, cream together butter, sugar, and eggs until very creamy and well blended. Add salt. Stir in flour, mixing to blend well. Add chocolate syrup, vanilla, and chopped nuts. Pour mixture into well-greased and lightly floured 9 inch square pan. Smooth the top. Bake at 350 degrees for about 35 minutes or until a stick inserted near center comes out clean. Cut into squares. Garnish with pecan or walnut halves or dust with powdered sugar.

Makes 16 to 18 brownies.

* * *

CHOW MEIN NOODLES CASSEROLE

Delores Storly Corbin— Deceased

2 cans cream of celery soup
2 lbs. ground beef
2 cans chicken with rice soup
1 onion, medium
2 cans vegetable soup
13 oz. chow mein noodles
Potato chips

Combine the soups and noodles in a casserole dish.

Brown beef and onion together and add to soup mixture. Put potato chips on top. Cover entire mixture with these potato chips. Bake for 1 hour at 350 degrees. (30 minutes for a 2 quart casserole)

*   *   *

COMPANY SALAD

Olive Brice Grace—Deceased

1 large head lettuce, shredded small
¼ cup green onions, finely chopped
¼ cup celery, finely chopped
1 6-oz.can water chestnuts, sliced
1 or 2 10-oz. pkgs. frozen peas—not thawed
1 ½ cup Best Foods mayonnaise
1 Tbsp. sugar
¾ lb. bacon, fried, crumbled
3 or 4 hard-boiled eggs, sliced
3 tomatoes, sliced
Romano and Parmesan cheese, grated

Place lettuce in large shallow 9 X 13 inch serving dish. Sprinkle green onion, celery and water chestnuts on top in layers. Break the peas apart and sprinkle on top. Spread the mayonnaise next like frosting. Sprinkle sugar on top of that.

Cover and refrigerate overnight.

Before serving, add bacon, sliced eggs, sliced tomatoes and grated cheeses on top. Do not stir.

Spoon out to serve on individual salad plates.

* * *

COWBOY COOKIES

Lyle Corbin Pierce—Deceased

1 cu p shortening
½ tsp. baking powder
1 cup white sugar
1 tsp. vanilla
1 cup brown sugar
2 cups flour
2 eggs
2 cups oatmeal
1 tsp. baking soda
1 pkg. chocolate chips
½ tsp. salt
½ cup chopped nuts

Mix all ingredients together in mixing bowl until cookie consistency is reached. Then place on floured surface and roll out until about 1/8 inch thick. Then cut out desired size and shape cookies using cookie cutters. Place on cookie sheet and bake at 350 degrees for 12 to 15 minutes

* * *

CRANBERRY BANANA TEA BREAD

Lulu Corbin Nash—Deceased

1¾ cup flour, sifted
½ tsp. salt
1¼ tsp. cream of tartar
¾ tsp. soda
⅓ cup butter
⅔ cup sugar
1 cup mashed bananas
2 eggs
1 cup jellied cranberry sauce, cubed

Cream butter, eggs, and sugar and beat well. Add dry ingredients alternately with mashed bananas. Gently fold in cubed jellied cranberries. Pour into greased bread pan.

Bake at 350 degrees for 1 hour.

*　*　*

CRANBERRY NUT BREAD

Neva Martin Hazen Ruth— Deceased

2 cups flour
1 well beaten egg
2 Tbsp. shortening
1½ tsp. baking powder
1 cup sugar
1 Tbsp. grated orange peel
1 tsp. salt
1 cup cranberries, chopped
½ tsp. soda
1 cup nuts
¾ cup orange juice

Mix together flour, sugar, baking powder, salt and soda. Add juice, egg, shortening and orange peel to dry ingredients. Mix until well blended. Stir in cranberries and nuts. Place in greased baking dish.

Bake at 350 degrees for 55 to 60 minutes.

* * *

DATE NUT BALLS

Lulu Corbin Nash—Deceased

½ cup butter
½ cup chopped dates
¾ cup sugar

Combine in fry pan and bring to a boil on low heat, then let cool. Beat 1 egg, add 1 tsp. vanilla and ½ tsp. salt. Stir into date mixture. Cook 2 minutes stirring while cooking.

Add ½ cup chopped nuts and 2 cups Rice Crispies—let cool.

Form into balls and roll in coconut.

*   *   *

DELUXE PEA SALAD

Jean Bruinier Nash—Deceased

1 bunch green onions
1 can turkey chunks
1 can water chestnuts, drained
1 pkg. frozen peas
and Cheese noodles

Mix with suitable amount of Mayonnaise and seasoning salt.

Serve...

*   *   *

DILL PICKLES

Lulu Corbin Nash—Deceased

Pack cucumbers into clean jars. Add sprigs of dill and pinch of alum in each jar.

Combine 4 qt. water, 2 cups salt and 1 qt vinegar.

Bring to a boil. Pour boiling mixture in jars and seal.

* * *

DOC'S PORK TENDERLOIN WITH ROSEMARY

Peggy Ann Chapman Corbin—Deceased

2 whole (½ to 1 lb) pork tenderloins
4 small onions cut into quarters
¼ cup butter
1½ cups of water
½ cup of Madeira wine
Salt and Pepper
3 cloves garlic, minced
1 Tbsp. rosemary leaves
1 Tbsp. oil
1 Tbsp. flour

Place tenderloins in roasting pan. Season to taste with salt and pepper. Sprinkle with minced garlic. Arrange onions around pork in pan. Melt 1 Tbsp. butter and combine with rosemary and oil.

Drizzle mixture over pork and onions. Roast at 325 degrees—about 45 minutes to 1 hour until tender and cooked through. Remove Tenderloins and onions from roasting pan. Deglaze pan with water.

Heat to boiling. Stir in wine. Blend together flour and remaining butter. Beat into sauce. Heat to boiling, stirring until thickened. Season to taste. Slice tenderloins and serve with onions and sauce. Serves 4 to 6.

* * *

DOC'S SAVORY TURKEY BURGERS

Peggy Chapman Corbin—Deceased

1 lb. raw ground turkey
¼ cup minced onion
Salt to taste
½ cup minced celery
¼ tsp. dried savory
Pinch of course pepper

Lightly toss ingredients together and shape into 4 burgers,

Broil or pan fry in a non-stick skillet sprayed with PAM.

Turn after 3 to 4 minutes and brown other side.

Burgers contain about 215 calories each.

*   *   *

DONUTS

Lulu Corbin Nash—Deceased

1-cup buttermilk
½ cup sweet milk
2 eggs, beaten
1-cup sugar
3 Tbsp. shortening, melted
Vanilla and nutmeg to taste
1 tsp. soda
1 tsp. baking powder
½ tsp. salt
2 cups flour
2 cups canola oil

Mix all of the ingredients together in a mixing bowl, then lay out on a sheet of cheese cloth that has been covered with flour, (enough so dough will not stick to the cheese cloth) and using a rolling pin, flatten until it is about a quarter of an inch thick. Using a floured donut cutter cut out all that you can and place cut out donuts into boiling cooking oil. (375 degrees) When donut is brown on both sides, remove and place on metal drying rack. Place two or three in the oil at a time.

* * *

DROP DONUTS

Alma Fehrs Corbin—Deceased

1 cup sugar
2 eggs, beaten
1 Tbsp. melted butter
1 cup sweet milk
3 cups flour
2 tsp. baking powder
1 tsp. vanilla

Cream all ingredients together. Drop by teaspoon in hot fat and fry until brown.

* * *

EGGPLANT AND SHRIMP

Jean Bruinier Nash—Deceased

Pare eggplant, cut into cubes, boil 15 minutes, mash, then combine with the following:

    1 cup cooked shrimp and
    1 finely chopped onion sautéed in 2 Tbsp. butter
    1 Tbsp. chopped parsley
    ½ cup course cracker crumbs
    1 egg yolk

Season to taste with salt and pepper. Put in greased casserole and bake in moderate hot oven at 375 degrees for 20 to 30 minutes.

* * *

FLUFFY POTATO CASSEROLE

Olive Brice Grace—Deceased

This was served at Father Martin's retirement celebration in Portland.

One of his nieces is responsible for this recipe.

    2 cups hot or cold mashed potatoes
    1 small onion, finely chopped
    Salt and pepper to taste
    1 8-oz. pkg. cream cheese at room temperature
    2 eggs
    2 Tbsp. flour

Beat at medium speed until blended, then on high speed until light and fluffy. Salt and pepper. Sprinkle 1 can French fried onions over top of mixture after you spoon it into a 9-inch squared greased dish. Bake uncovered at 300 degrees for 35 minutes.

For a double recipe, bake at 300 degrees for 1 hour 10 minutes in a 9 x 13 inch pan. If onions start to brown too quickly, cover with foil.

* * *

FROZEN SLAW

Lulu Corbin Nash—Deceased

Grind cabbage, sprinkle with salt, let stand
Drain well, add green pepper.
Grind one little carrot, if desired

DRESSING: add 2 cups of sugar, 1 cup of vinegar, 1 tsp. celery seed and 1 tsp. mustard seeds

Put in container and let stand in refrigerator for a few days.

It may freeze

* * *

FUDGE COOKIES

Alma Fehrs Corbin—Deceased

1 cup shortening
2 squares chocolate, melted
1¼ cups brown sugar
1 tsp. baking powder
2 eggs
2 cups flour
½ cup milk
½ cup nut meats (optional)

Mix ingredients in order given by column, left column first. Drop on cookie sheet. Bake at 350 degrees in oven for 10 minutes.

* * *

GINGERED PORK ROAST

Peggy Ann Chapman Corbin—Deceased

Ginger root
1 boneless pork loin roast (4 to 5 lbs.)
1 pkg. (3 oz.) orange gelatin
1 Tbsp. grated orange peel
Salt and pepper
1½ cups orange juice
1 cup molasses
¾ tsp. salt

Peel ginger root and cut off 3 to 4 slices. Stack slices and cut into slivers. With tip of sharp knife, make incisions about 2 inches apart over entire surface of roast. Insert ginger slivers into each slit. Season with salt and pepper to taste.

Place on rack in open roasting pan and insert meat thermometer. Roast uncovered at 325 degrees 40 to 45 minutes per pound or to internal temperature of 160 degrees. Bring orange juice to boil in sauce pan. Stir in gelatin, orange peel, molasses, salt and 1 Tbsp. grated ginger root. About 1 hour before end of roasting, brush pork with ½ cup sauce. Remove roast from oven and allow to stand for 20 minutes before carving. Add pan drippings to sauce, reheat, strain and serve with meat. This serves 8 to 10 persons.

* * *

GLAZED SPUD NUTS

Alma Fehrs Corbin—Deceased

Part 1:
⅛ cup sugar
¼ cup mashed potatoes
½ cup lard or Crisco
1 egg, beaten

Part II:
Add: 4 cups flour (measured after sifting), and pinch of salt. Mix as pie crust

Part III:
2 yeast cakes (compressed or granular) dissolved in ½ cup water (good measure)
½ cup milk—scalded and cooled to lukewarm temperature.

Add to the above mixture and handle lightly. Roll out to ½ inch thick, cut with doughnut cutter and let rise about one hour. Fry in deep fat which is slightly hotter than for other doughnuts. Glaze while hot with mixture of cold water and powdered sugar. Let drip off from cake cooler or grate.
It if gets too thick, thin with water.

* * *

GOULASH

Alma Fehrs Corbin—Deceased

Add 1 can of tomatoes (1 lb), and 1 ½ lbs lean stewing beef and 2 cups boiling water. Cover tightly. Reduce heat and simmer for 1 ½ hours or until meat is almost tender.

Sift together:
¼ cup sifted regular flour
½ tsp salt
¼ tsp. pepper
Add 1 - 2 Tbsp. paprika
Salt to taste
Pepper to taste
Roll meat in flour mixture.

Heat in a Dutch oven or large sauce pan. Add 1 to 2 Tbsp. fat. Then add meat. Cook over medium heat until meat is browned, turning frequently to brown evenly.

Add 1 cup chopped onions and cook over medium heat until lightly browned.

Cook in boiling salted water until tender:
3½ cups noodles.

Drain well. Rinse with cold water. Drain. Add meat mixture. Mix well. Makes about 5 servings.

* * *

GRANDMA CORBIN'S CHOCOLATE CAKE

Ruth Corbin Grave—Deceased

This was a recipe used often by my Mother, Alma Fehrs Corbin

    2 eggs, beaten
    ¾ cup sugar
    ½ cup cocoa
    Pinch of salt
    1 cup sour cream or ½ cup shortening
    1 tsp baking powder
    1 tsp. soda
    1 to 2 cups flour, adding more liquid (milk) if too thick.

Mix all ingredients together and beat well. When "Ma" made this cake she would add part of a cup of coffee, little dabs of jelly out of jars, and add a teaspoonful or two of sauce (apple or whatever) Bake in a long pan at medium temperature (350 degrees) until top springs back up when touched with fingertip. Frost with favorite frosting after cake has cooled, and serve with Whipped topping.

*   *   *

GRANDMA CORBIN'S PEA SALAD

Ruth Corbin Graves—Deceased

This recipe was used by my Mother, Alma Fehrs Corbin.

When Ma made this salad dressing, she prepared it in a small pan set on top of the open tea kettle on the old wood stove—thus creating a double boiler.

    2 cans sweet peas, drained
    3 or 4 eggs, boiled, peeled, chopped
    ½ cup {approx} American cheese, diced
    Add to taste— Chopped sweet pickle or relish

Mix with salad dressing to moisten. Ma always made her own salad dressing with egg yolk, vinegar, milk, mustard, and whatever....

This was always her favorite for Sunday Dinner.

* * *

HEARTY PEA, BEAN, AND BARLEY SOUP

Peggy Ann Chapman Corbin—Deceased

½ cup barley
1 cup navy dried beans
1 cup dried split peas
2 lbs. short ribs
2 onions, diced
2 stalks celery, thinly sliced
8 carrots, peeled, thinly sliced
2 bay leaves, crumbled
1 parsnip, peeled, thinly sliced
1 rutabaga, peeled, diced
1 tsp. dried thyme
½ tsp. dried marjoram
1 16-oz. can whole peeled tomatoes
Salt and pepper

Cover barley, beans and split peas with 3 qt. of water and soak at least 4 hours or overnight. Place short ribs, onions, celery, carrots, parsnips and rutabaga in large pot. Add 10 to 12 cups of water or enough to cover. Drain barley, beans and peas and add to pot with bay leaves, thyme and marjoram. Mix well. Season to taste with salt and pepper. Add un-drained tomatoes. Bring to boil, lower heat and simmer gently until barley, beans and peas are tender, usually 1 to 1 ½ hours.

If serving in mugs, remove meat from bones and serve pieces or meat with soup.

Makes about 12 servings. Is best after setting for a day.

*   *   *

HOME MADE SAUSAGE

Jean Bruinier Nash—Deceased

5 lbs. cheap hamburger
5 rounded tsp. Morton Quick Tender Salt
2½ tsp. mustard seed
2½ tsp. course ground pepper
2½ tsp. garlic salt
1 tsp. hickory smoke salt

First day: Mix and refrigerate

Second day: mix and refrigerate

Third day: Shape into 5 rolls, place in boiler pan on bottom oven rack.

Bake at 140 degrees for 8 hours, turning the rolls every 2 hours. It forms its own casing and doesn't crumble. Let cool and slice to suit.

Tastes real good.

*   *   *

INFORMATION ON MAKING STOCK

Peggy Chapman Corbin—Deceased

1} To adjust canned stock—Dilute the concentrated soup with water to reduce the salt content, Add onion, garlic, leek, carrot, celery, tomato, parsley, whole peppercorns, and allspice berries.

Brink stock to a boil, simmer for 30 minutes or longer. Strain.

Add a healthy shot of bourbon whiskey to reinforce flavor.

2} Freeze stock in ice cube trays.

3} Pot in which you cook stock should be narrow, rather than wide, so all ingredients steep in the liquid, and, evaporation is kept to a minimum.

4} Always roast bones or meat with which stock is flavored.

5} Skim scum constantly.

6} Add vegetables such as onions and parsnips but do not peel them. The skins add color.

7} Add all fresh herbs, except parsley, at the point when stock is half cooked so they do not overpower the stock.

8} Stock should simmer, but never boil.

9} Expect only one-half the amount of liquid you begin with.

* * *

IRISH SODA BREAD

Neva Martin Hazen Ruth—Deceased

3 cups flour
1½ cups seedless raisins
⅓ cup sugar
1¾ cup buttermilk
2 tsp. baking powder
2 eggs, beaten
1 tsp. soda
2 Tbsp. oil
1 tsp. salt
½ cup chopped nuts

Sift flour, sugar, baking powder, soda, and salt into large bowl. Stir in raisins and nuts. Combine milk, eggs, and oil and add to other mixture. Mix until flour is moistened. Place in loaf pan. Bake at 350 degrees for one hour.

* * *

IRISH STEW

Peggy Ann Chapman Corbin—Deceased

8 lbs. lean lamb or beef
1½ cup of all-purpose flour
1 Tbsp. salt
½ tsp. pepper
6 to 8 Tbsp. vegetable oil
4 onions, peeled, diced
2 Tbsp. sugar
1 16-oz.can tomato puree
6 cups dry red wine (or enough to cover ⅔ of meat
1 tsp. dried thyme
2 Tbsp. dried basil
4 cloves garlic, peeled, crushed
2 lbs. small fresh mushrooms
4 tsp. grated orange peel
2 lbs. frozen baby carrots or whole carrots, peeled &
cut into 2-inch lengths 1 inch wide.

Pat meat dry, then dredge in flour that has been mixed with salt and pepper. In large heavy casserole or Dutch oven, heat oil. Add meat in single layer batches and sauté over medium high heat until browned on all sides. Remove meat as it browns. When all meat has been browned and removed, add onions and sugar in pan drippings. Sauté, stirring constantly until glazed and lightly browned, adding more oil if needed. Drain off any excess fat. Add wine to pan and cook over medium heat 2 minutes, stirring constantly and scraping up any browned bits from bottom of pan. Stir in tomato puree.
Serves 16.

* * *

JOHN'S RHUBARB MUFFINS

John Corbin Brice—Deceased

Makes 10 large or 18 regular sized muffins.
Preheat oven to 375 degrees.

1¼ cups brown sugar
½ cup oil (any cooking oil)
1 egg
1 cup sour milk
½ cup chopped nuts
2½ cups flour
1 tsp. soda
1 tsp. baking powder
½ tsp. salt
1½ cups diced rhubarbs

Mix ingredients in order shown. spray muffin pan (any type) with PAM. Fill muffin cups ⅔ full. For large muffins, bake at 375 degrees for 35 minutes. For small muffins, bake at 375 degrees for 25 minutes.

*   *   *

KING'S DELIGHT BARS

Ruth Corbin Graves—Deceased

First layer:
    ½ cup brown sugar
    1 cup flour
    ½ cup margarine
Mix ingredients together and put in 9 x 13 inch pan.
Bake at 350 degrees for 10 minutes.
Then set aside until second layer is ready to be poured over first layer.
Second layer:
    2 eggs
    ½ tsp. salt
    1 cup nutmeats
    1 cup chocolate chips
    1½ tsp. vanilla
    1 cup brown sugar
    1 tsp. baking powder

Mix ingredients together and pour over first layer. Bake at 350 degrees for 25 minutes.

*　*　*

LAYER MEXICAN DIP

Linda Kirk Pierce—Deceased

2 8-oz.ctns. of avocado dip
2 15-oz.cans refried beans
1 12-oz.pkg. shredded cheddar cheese
2 medium tomatoes, chopped
2 8-oz.ctns. sour cream {Can use plain yogurt}
1 pkg. taco seasoning mix
1 4-oz.can chopped ripe olives
2 bunches of green onions, chopped

In a 9 by 13 inch pan, layer beans and avocado dip.

Combine sour cream and taco seasoning and layer on top of avocado dip. Sprinkle ½ of cheese, then top with olives, tomato, and onion. Add remaining cheese.

Then pass the Tortilla chips.

* * *

LOU'S WHITE SUGAR COOKIES

Lulu Corbin Nash—Deceased

1 cup sugar—scant
½ tsp. almond extract
1 cup shortening
2 cups flour
1 egg
½ tsp. soda
¼ tsp. salt
½ tsp. cream of tarter
½ tsp. vanilla

Mix all of the above ingredients together and make it into a doughy kind of material. Then do as it is indicated below.

Roll into balls. Dip in sugar and flatten.

Optional: May roll or use press.

Bake at 375 degrees for 8 to 10 minutes.

*   *   *

MAC'S CIOPPINO

Margaret Ann Chapman Corbin (MAC)—Deceased

1 15 oz. can tomato sauce
1 chopped onion
1 6 oz. can tomato paste
2 Tbsp. olive oil
2 cups water
½ tsp. thyme
1 bay leaf
¼ tsp. oregano
½ tsp. black pepper

Sauté onions in olive oil. Place in large pot and add the rest of the above ingredients. Simmer for 2 hours. Then add the following:

1 lb. light-fleshed fish
1 lb. shrimp
1 can minced clams
1 lb. scallops
1 lb. crab meat

Cook about 15 minutes. Serve with crusty bread.

* * *

MEAT LOAF

Alma Fehrs Corbin—Deceased

1½ lb. ground beef
½ lb. ground pork
¼ cup finely chopped onion
2 tsp. salt
¼ tsp. pepper
¼ tsp. sage
¼ tsp. poultry seasoning
1 Tbsp. Worcestershire sauce
2 eggs
1 cup tomato juice
4 slices bread

Combine meat with onions and seasonings. Beat eggs and add to tomato juice. Cube bread and soak in the liquid mixture. beat well. Add to meat and mix lightly. Pack into a 5x9 inch meat loaf pan and bake at 350 degrees for 1¼ hours. Let loaf stand for 10 minutes, then drain off liquid and turn out of pan. Spread with catsup or hot tomato juice.

If desired, the loaf may be spread with ⅓ cup catsup before baking. This adds moisture and interesting flavor.

* * *

MEXICAN BEEF STIR-FRY

Peggy Ann Chapman Corbin-Deceased

1 lb. beef flank steak
2 Tbsp. oil
1 tsp. ground cumin
1 tsp. garlic salt
1 tsp. crushed oregano
1 medium onion, chopped
1 sweet red pepper, cut into thin strips
1 to 2 jalapeno chilies, seeded and cut into slivers

Cut beef flank steak diagonally across grain into $\frac{1}{8}$ inch thick slices. Combine oil, cumin, garlic salt, and oregano. Using medium-high heat, heat 1 Tbsp. oil mixture in a Wok or large non-stick Skillet. Then add red pepper, onion and jalapeno chili and stir-fry this mixture 2 to 3 minutes, or until tender-crisp. Remove from pan and reserve.

In remaining oil mixture, stir-fry beef strips, one-half at a time, 1 to 2 minutes. Then combine all the beef and vegetables in the Wok or Skillet and heat through. Serves 4.

* * *

MINT FUDGE SAUCE

Peggy Chapman Corbin—Deceased

4 (1-oz) squares of unsweetened chocolate
¼ cup plus 2 Tbsp. butter or margarine
⅔ cup finely crushed peppermint
¾ cup milk
1 cup sugar
Dash of salt

Combine chocolate and milk in the top of a double boiler. Place over simmering water and stir frequently until chocolate melts and mixture is well blended. Stir in sugar and salt, cook about 5 minutes or until sugar is slightly thickened. Remove from heat, and add butter, stirring gently until butter melts.

Serve warm or cool completely and spoon into decorative jars.

Cover tightly and refrigerate up to 3 weeks. Makes 2½ cups.

*   *   *

MOUND BARS

Linda Kirk Pierce—Deceased

½ cup melted butter
2 cups graham cracker crumbs
¼ cup sugar

Combine ingredients, pat into 9 by 13 inch pan. Bake for ten minutes at 350 degrees. Combine and mix well one 7-oz.pkg. Angel Flake Coconut and one can Eagle brand condensed milk. Pour over the baked warm crust and bake an additional 15 minutes at 350 degrees. Then Spread on frosting.

The Frosting recipe:
Combine 1⅓ cups sugar, 6 Tbsp. milk, and six Tbsp. margarine. Boil for ½ minute, remove from heat and add ½ cup chocolate chips and ½ cup chopped nuts.

For an alternate frosting: Melt 1 pkg. chocolate chips and add ½ Tbsp. peanut butter.

*   *   *

NUTMEG COOKIE LOGS

Olive Brice Grace—Deceased

Sift together: 3 cups flour and 1 tsp. nutmeg
Cream: 1 cup butter added gradually to ¾ cup sugar
Blend: 1 unbeaten egg, 2 tsp. vanilla and 2 tsp. rum flavoring.

Add gradually the dry ingredients and mix thoroughly. Shape dough on lightly floured surface into long rolls ½ inch in diameter.

Cut into 3 inch lengths. Place on ungreased baking sheets.

Bake at 350 degrees for 12 to 15 minutes. Cool, spread frosting on tops and sides of cookie. Mark frosting with tines of a fork to resemble bark. Sprinkle lightly with nutmeg.

To Make the Frosting:

Cream 3 Tbsp. butter with ½ tsp vanilla and 1 tsp. rum flavoring. Blend in ½ cup sifted powdered sugar, beating well. Add 2 cups additional sifted confectioners (powdered) sugar alternately with 2 to 3 Tbsp. undulated evaporated milk or cream, beating well after each addition until spreading consistency is achieved.

* * *

MICROWAVE OVEN PEANUT BRITTLE

Jean Bruinier Nash—Deceased

1 cup sugar
½ cup corn syrup
Combine above and microwave for four minutes.
Add 1 cup peanuts and microwave 4 minutes more.
Add 1 Tbsp. butter, stir 2 minutes, stir in 1 tsp. baking soda and 1 tsp. vanilla.

Spread on well-greased cookie sheet to cool. Break into bite size pieces.

* * *

MINCE MEAT

Lulu Corbin Nash—Deceased

3 bowls of chopped meat
4 bowls sugar
5 bowls chopped apples
2 Tbsp. cinnamon
2 bowls raisins
1 Tbsp. cloves
½ bowl molasses
1 Tbsp. salt
1 bowl vinegar
1 Tbsp. pepper
1 bowl cider
3 lemons

Mix all but the meat and spices—boil until tender.
Add meat, seal and process.

*   *   *

MOTHERS BANANA BREAD

Neva Martin Hazen Ruth—Deceased

1 cup sugar
1 tsp. soda
2 cups flour
½ cup shortening
2 eggs, beaten
Add nuts and salt
3 bananas—at least a cup of them

Cream sugar and shortening. Add whole beaten eggs and continue creaming. Mash bananas and add to mixture. Add dry ingredients, then the nuts. Pour in greased loaf pans. Bake at 350 degrees for 1 hour.

* * *

NUTMEG COOKIE LOGS

Olive Brice Grace—Deceased

These are my son's favorite Christmas cookies.

Sift together: 3 cups flour & 1 tsp. nutmeg.
Cream: 1 cup butter added gradually to ¾ cup sugar.
Blend: 1 unbeaten egg, 2 tsp. vanilla, and 2 tsp. rum flavoring.

Add gradually the dry ingredients and mix thoroughly. Shape dough on lightly floured surface into long rolls ½ inch in diameter. Cut into 3-inch lengths. Place on ungreased baking sheets. Bake at 350 degrees for 12 to 15 minutes. Cool, then spread frosting on tops and sides of cookie. Mark frosting with tines of fork to resemble bark. Sprinkle lightly with nutmeg.

FROSTING: Cream 3 Tbsp. butter with ½ tsp. vanilla and 1 tsp. rum flavoring. Blend in ½ cup sifted powdered sugar, beating well.

Add 2 cups additional sifted confectioners {powdered} sugar alternately with 2 to 3 Tbsp. undiluted evaporated milk, or cream, beating well after each addition until spreading consistency is achieved.

*   *   *

OATMEAL COOKIES

Alma Fehrs Corbin—Deceased

1 cup flour, sifted
1 cup brown sugar
1 tsp. baking powder
2 eggs
⅓ cup milk
½ tsp. salt
3 cups oatmeal
1 tsp. cinnamon
¼ tsp. nutmeg
¾ cup shortening
1 cup raisins

Sift together dry ingredients into mixing bowl. Add shortening, brown sugar and ½ of the milk. Beat 2 minutes. Fold in the remaining milk, raisins and rolled oats. Drop from teaspoon onto greased baking sheet and bake 12 to 15 minutes. Makes 4 dozen.

* * *

ORANGE CHEESECAKE (Microwave)

Peggy Ann Chapman Corbin—Deceased

3 Tbsp. butter or margarine
1 beaten egg
2/3 cup finely crushed graham crackers
1/3 cup sugar
1 Tbsp. sugar
2 (3 oz.) pkg. cream cheese
3 Tbsp. orange juice
1/4 tsp. vanilla
1 tsp. finely shredded orange peel
1/3 cup dairy sour cream
1/4 cup orange marmalade

For crust, in a 7 inch pie plate cook butter or margarine, uncovered, on 100 % power (high) for 45 to 60 seconds or until melted. Add crushed graham crackers and 1 Tbsp. sugar. Stir until all is moistened. Press mixture firmly against bottom and sides of pie plate. Cook, uncovered, on high for 1 to 1½ minutes or until set, giving pie plate a half-turn after 30 seconds. Set aside.

In microwave-safe mixing bowl cook cream cheese, uncovered, on 50% power (medium) for 1 to 1½ minutes or until softened. Stir in beaten egg, 1/3 cup sugar, and sour cream until mixture is smooth.

Add orange peel, orange juice, and vanilla. Mix well. Pour cream cheese mixture into crust. Cook, uncovered, on medium power (50%) for 8 to 10 minutes or until a knife inserted 1 inch from edge comes out clean, giving pie plate a quarter turn every 2 minutes.

Center will be slightly set but not firm. Cool slightly.

Meanwhile, in a small microwave-safe bowl or custard cup, cook orange marmalade on 100% power (high) for 30 to 60 seconds or until warm. Spoon over top of cheesecake. Cool. Refrigerate at least 3 hours or until set. Makes 6 servings.

* * *

ORANGE PINEAPPLE DESSERT

Ruth Corbin Graves—Deceased

1 3-oz. pkg. orange-pineapple Jell-O
1 can {15½ oz.} crushed pineapple

Prepare Jell-O according to pkg. instructions. Allow Jell-O to set.

Drain off canned pineapple juice and save it for pudding recipe. Spread drained pineapple over the Jell-O.

For Pudding Recipe—combine:
   1 cup pineapple juice
   3 Tbsp. cornstarch
   ½ cup sugar
   1 egg yolk

Cook pudding ingredients together until thick and creamy. Let cool. When cool, spread over the pineapple, then add a layer of miniature marshmallows.

Serve with whipped topping with a garnish of grated cheddar cheese.

* * *

ORANGE SUNBEAMS

(For a Diabetic diet)
Lulu Corbin Nash—Deceased

(For a Diabetic diet)
    1½ cups flour
    1 tsp. baking powder
    ⅓ cup raisins
    3 tsp. grated orange rind
    1½ tsp. liquid sweetener
    ¼ tsp. salt
    ½ cup butter
    1 unbeaten egg
    2 Tbsp. orange juice

Sift flour, baking powder and salt into a bowl, add butter, egg, orange juice, rind, and sweetener. Mix well. Add raisins. Drop by teaspoon onto greased cookie sheet.

Bake in oven at 375 degrees for 12 to 15 minutes.

*   *   *

OSSO BUCCO

Peggy Ann Corbin—Deceased

3 lbs. lean veal chunks or shanks
¼ cup flour
½ tsp. freshly ground black pepper
2 tsp. salt
¾ cup chopped onions
1 rib celery, chopped
1 Tbsp. tomato paste
2 Tbsp. minced parsley
2 Tbsp. grated lemon rind
2 Tbsp. olive oil
2 Tbsp. butter
¼ tsp. rosemary
¼ cup white wine
½ cup water
1 clove garlic, minced
¼ cup grated carrots

Roll veal lightly in the flour. Heat the oil and butter in a Dutch oven or heavy saucepan. Brown veal in it. Sprinkle with salt, pepper and the rosemary. Add onions, carrots, and celery. Cook 5 minutes. Add the wine and cook until evaporated. Mix in the tomato paste and water. Cover and cook over low heat 2 hours or until tender. Add small amounts of boiling water from time to time, if necessary. Mix together the lemon rind, garlic, and parsley. Stir into gravy. Recover and cook another 5 minutes longer. Serve with rice. Serves 6.

* * *

OVEN PORK CHOPS

Catherin Nash Bosmoe—Deceased

1 can cream of chicken soup
2 Tbsp. Worcestershire sauce
1 medium onion, sliced
6 pork chops
3 Tbsp. catsup

Brown pork chops in a frying pan, then place in a casserole covering chops with sliced onions. Mix the soup, sauce, and catsup. Pour over the chops. Bake covered for 1 hour in 350 degree oven. Gravy from this is delicious.

* * *

PEACH UPSIDE-DOWN CAKE

Alma Fehrs Corbin—Deceased

1 pint frozen or canned peaches
¼ cup butter
⅔ cup light brown sugar, firmly packed
Combine the following ingredients to make the cake batter
1½ cups flour
2 tsp. baking powder
½ tsp. salt
½ cup granulated sugar
¼ cup butter
2 eggs, beaten
¼ tsp. almond extract
½ cup milk

Melt brown sugar and butter in a 9 inch baking pan. Arrange peaches in bottom of pan. Pour cake batter over peaches and bake in a moderated oven at 375 degrees for about 40 minutes, or until cake springs back when touched with finger. Cool ten minutes in pan, then turn upside-down on a large serving plate.

* * *

PEANUT BRITTLE

Olive Brice Grace—Deceased

Olive made this for her neighbors at Christmas time. The directions must be followed very carefully.

    1 cup sugar
    ¼ tsp baking soda
    ¼ cup water
    A few drops vanilla
    ¼ cup white Karo syrup
    2 Tbsp. margarine
    ¾ cup raw shelled Spanish peanuts
    ½ tsp. salt

Put the sugar, water and Karo syrup into a 1-quart pan on medium heat. When it boils up the first time, wash the sugar crystals down from the side of the pot and the stirring paddle. Stir in the margarine. Cook to 250 degrees without further stirring. Then stir in the peanuts and continue stirring gently until the thermometer reads 320 degrees. Take from the stove and stir in the salt, baking soda and vanilla. Pour onto greased baking sheet. Wait a few minutes for it to cool slightly. Loosen from sheet, turn it over and stretch it out as thinly as possible (with buttered fingers). Let cool until hard brittle breaks. To keep from sticking, store in air tight jar or tin or plastic bag.

* * *

PEPPERMINT POUND CAKE

Peggy Ann Corbin—Deceased

1 (16 oz.) pkg. pound cake mix
¼ cup butter
½ to ¾ tsp. peppermint extract
2 eggs, beaten
12 drops red food coloring
½ cup water
Mint Fudge Sauce

Cream butter in large mixing bowl, add eggs, one at a time, beating well after each addition. Add water and peppermint extract, beating well. Add pound cake mix, and beat at medium speed of an electric mixer 3 minutes, scraping bowl often. Drop red food coloring over surface of batter, stir gently just to swirl color.

Bake at 350 degrees for 35 minutes or until wooden pick inserted in center comes out clean. Let cool in pan 10 minutes, remove from pan, and cool completely on wire rack.

Serve with Mint Fudge Sauce.

Makes one 8 inch cake.

*   *   *

PEPPER STEAK

Peggy Ann Corbin—Deceased

2 lbs. beef top round
1 can (6-oz) sliced mushrooms or ½ lb. fresh mushrooms, sliced
½ tsp. black pepper
1 clove garlic, minced
5 to 6 dashes curry powder
Chicken or beef stock
¼ cup olive oil
1 clove garlic
2 large green peppers
2 large onions
2 tsp. salt
¾ cup dry red wine

Trim fat from meat. Cut meat into ½ inch strips. Heat 2 Tbsp. olive oil and whole garlic in skillet add meat and brown all sides, stirring occasionally. Discard garlic. Meanwhile, cut green peppers into thin strips and chop onions coarsely. Sauté onions and green peppers in remaining 2 Tbsp. olive oil in another skillet until tender but not brown.

Add mushrooms, pepper, salt, and minced garlic. Add vegetables to meat, then add wine. Cover and simmer 30 minutes. Stir in curry powder and simmer 1 hour longer. If mixture needs more liquid, add chicken or beef broth.

This will serve 8 easily.

* * *

PINEAPPLE-GLAZED APPLE PIE

Peggy Chapman Corbin—Deceased

1 ½ cups unsweetened pineapple juice
7 tart medium apples, peeled, cored and cut in wedges
(7 cups)
1 Tbsp. butter or margarine
1 baked 9-inch single-crust pie shell, cooled
¾ cup sugar
3 Tbsp. cornstarch
½ tsp. vanilla
¼ tsp. salt

In a large saucepan combine 1 ¼ cups of pineapple juice and the sugar. Bring to boiling, add apple wedges. Simmer, covered, 3 to 4 minutes or till apples are tender but not soft. With slotted spoon, lift apples from pineapple liquid; set apples aside to drain. Blend the remaining ¼ cup pineapple juice slowly into cornstarch, add to hot pineapple liquid in saucepan. Cook and stir until mixture thickens and bubbles. cook 1 minute more. Remove from heat. Stir in the butter or margarine, vanilla, and salt. Cover and cool 30 minutes without stirring. Pour half the pineapple mixture into the baked pie shell, spreading to cover the bottom. Arrange cooked apples atop. Spoon remaining mixture over apples. Cover and refrigerate until chilled. Before serving, garnish center of pie with whipped cream and chopped macadamia nuts, if desired.

* * *

PINK PICKLED EGGS

Peggy Chapman Corbin—Deceased

6 hard-boiled eggs, shelled
¾ cup juice drained from canned or cooked beets
¼ tsp. allspice
Dash black pepper
½ cup dry red wine
¾ cup vinegar
1 bay leaf
¾ tsp. salt
1 clove garlic, crushed

Place eggs in quart jar. Combine beet juice, wine, vinegar, bay leaf, allspice, salt, pepper and garlic in sauce pan. Heat but do not allow to boil. Pour hot liquid over eggs. Cool, then cover and refrigerate overnight, or longer, if desired.

* * *

POPCORN BALLS

Olive Brice Grace—Deceased

Those who lived in South Dakota will remember my mother's popcorn balls. This is the recipe she gave me many years ago, minus instructions. But I do remember the instructions to put the soda in after the syrup was cooked and off of the stove. When I would ask how much popcorn to use, she would say "A bowl full".

1 cup molasses
2 cups sugar
1 Tbsp. butter
2 Tbsp. vinegar
½ tsp. soda

EDITORS NOTE: In Alma Fehrs Corbin's "York Thursday Club Cook Book" {The club was a group of ladies in and around Lily, York Township, South Dakota} we found the following instructions by Vivian Corbin Brice for her popcorn ball recipe.

Boil until mixture cracks in cold water.

Add ½ tsp soda, stir well. Pour over corn and shape into balls.

Enough for a small dishpan full of popped corn.

The Cookbook indicated light or dark syrup could be substituted for molasses

* * *

POPPY SEED CAKE

Olive Brice Grace—Deceased

1 pkg. white cake mix
1 pkg. poppy seeds
1 pkg. vanilla instant pudding
1 cup water
4 eggs
½ cup oil

Combine everything together in a mixing bowl and mix together for 5 minutes. Pour in a Bundt pan. Bake 45 to 55 minutes at 350 degrees.

* * *

POTATO REFRIGERATOR ROLLS

Olive Brice Grace—Deceased

1 cup mashed potatoes
½ cup sugar
1 cup scalded milk
2 tsp. salt
2 pkg. yeast, dissolved in ½ cup water
2 eggs, beaten
5½ cups flour (approx.)

Add all ingredients to cool scalded milk, adding flour last. Dough should be a little sticky. Can be kept in refrigerator 3 or 4 days. Punch down when it rises too much. Can be made any shape. Makes 3 dozen crescent rolls or 2 large pans of cinnamon rolls. Also freezes well after baking.

May glaze with powdered sugar and water mixture. Bake at 425 degrees for 15 to 20 minutes.

* * *

PORK CASSEROLE

Alma Fehrs Corbin—Deceased

1½ lbs. lean pork, cut in 1 inch pieces
1 cup carrots, diced
½ Tbsp. spry or lard
½ cup sifted all-purpose flour
1½ cups diced potatoes
¼ Tbsp. finely chopped onions
¾ cup green lima beans
¾ tsp. salt
¼ tsp. pepper
1½ cups water
½ Tbsp. salt
1½ cups sour cream

Sprinkle meat with salt and pepper. Brown the meat in fat. Add the water, cover and simmer until meat is tender. Meanwhile cook the carrots until tender. Combine flour, sour cream, beat until smooth. Blend with meat mixture. Add vegetables and salt, mix all well. Put in greased casserole. Bake covered at 375 degrees for one hour, then bake uncovered about 30minutes to brown the top.

*   *   *

PORK CHOPS AND STUFFING

Linda Kirk Pierce—Deceased

4 to 6 pork chops
¼ cup water
3 cups soft bread cubes
¼ tsp. poultry seasoning
2 Tbsp. chopped onions
¼ cup melted butter
1 can cream of mushroom soup
⅓ cup water

Brown chops on both sides. Place in shallow baking dish. Lightly mix bread cubes, onion, butter, ¼ cup water and poultry seasoning.

Place a mound of stuffing on each chop. Blend soup and ⅓ cup water, pour over top of chops.

Bake in a 350 Degree oven for one hour or until tender.

*   *   *

POT OF BEANS

Ruth Corbin Graves—Deceased

2 lbs. dry pinto beans freshly picked from your garden.

Pick over beans and remove small rocks from hulling. Wash beans and cover with cold water and let soak for several hours. Drain and cover with fresh water and put on to cook. When about ½ cooked. put in ham bone or ham in sizable chunks, add 4 to 5 Tbsp. brown sugar or molasses, salt to taste, and pepper. Continue cooking until flavors are well blended and beans and meat are done. Serve with Cornbread and fried taters and diced onions on a cold winter's night and this is sure to please everyone.

* * *

PUMPKIN CAKE

Linda Kirk Pierce—Deceased

1 yellow cake mix
3 eggs
½ cup melted butter
2 tsp. cinnamon
1 egg
½ cup brown sugar
1 quart can pumpkin
⅔ cup milk
½ cup sugar
¼ cup soft butter
⅔ cup chopped walnuts

Reserving 1 cup of cake mix for top, combine rest of cake mix, melted butter and 1 egg: then press into 9 by 13 inch pan that has been greased with Crisco. Combine pumpkin, 3 eggs, cinnamon, brown sugar, and milk—then pour on top of crust.

Mix reserved cake mix, sugar, soft butter and walnuts with a fork— then sprinkle on top of pumpkin mixture.

Bake at 350 degrees for 50 to 60 minutes

* * *

PUMPKIN COOKIES

Catherin Nash Bosmoe—Deceased

1 cup sugar
1 tsp. cinnamon
½ cup butter
1 tsp. baking powder
1 egg
½ cup dates, chopped
1 cup pumpkin
½ cup nuts, chopped
1 tsp. vanilla
2 cups flour

Mix in order given. Bake at 350 degrees for 10 minutes. Cool and frost with powdered sugar frosting using orange juice.

Makes 3 dozen cookies.

* * *

QUEEN—ESTER'S SEED CAKE

Peggy Chapman Corbin—Deceased

1 cup margarine
1²/₃ cups sugar
1 tsp. vanilla
8 egg whites
2²/₃ cups sifted cake flour
¼ tsp. ground ginger
½ tsp. cream of tartar
¼ tsp. salt
Grated peel of 1 lemon
1 Tbsp. poppy seeds
1 Tbsp. sesame seeds
1 Tbsp. caraway seeds
Powdered sugar

Beat margarine and ²/₃ cup sugar in large bowl until creamy. Add vanilla and beat well. Gradually beat into the mixture 1²/₃ cups flour and the ground ginger. Set aside.

Beat egg whites with cream of tartar and salt in large mixing bowl until foamy. Gradually add remaining 1 cup sugar and beat into stiff peaks. Add ¼ cup of this meringue to margarine mixture, blending to lighten batter. Gently but thoroughly fold margarine mixture into remaining meringue. Sift remaining 1 cup flour into batter and gently fold.

Gently fold in lemon peel and seeds. DO NOT OVER MIX. Spoon batter into greased and floured 10 inch tube pan. Bake at 350 degrees for 45 minutes or until wood pick inserted in middle comes out clean. Cool pan 15 minutes, then turn out onto rack. Just before serving, dust with powdered sugar.

Makes 1 cake.

* * *

QUICK DESSERT

Linda Kirk Pierce—Deceased

1 white or yellow cake mix
2 cans of cherry pie filling
½ cup butter, melted

Place cherries in 9 by 13 inch pan. Sprinkle dry cake mix over top.

Sprinkle with butter.

Bake in 350 degree oven for 40 minutes.

*   *   *

RAISIN DATE NUT COOKIES

Alma Fehrs Corbin—Deceased

Mix 2 cups raisins
¼ cup dates
2 cups water
Boil down until 1 cup of juice mixture remains. Let cool, add 1 tsp. soda and cream with the following:
⅔ cup Crisco or lard
1 cup white sugar
1 cup brown sugar
1 tsp. cinnamon
½ tsp. cloves
2 eggs, beaten
¼ tsp. salt
1 tsp. vanilla
½ cup sour cream
½ cup chopped nuts
3½ cups flour

Mix everything together and Drop by teaspoon on a cookie sheet.

Bake in a 375 degree oven.

For the Frosting, combine and bring to boil:
½ cup sugar
½ cup milk
1 Tbsp. (heaping) Crisco or butter

Remove from heat add powdered sugar to obtain desired consistency.

* * *

RAMEN NOODLE SALAD

Olive Brice Grace—Deceased

2 Tbsp. sesame seed, toasted
½ cup slivered almonds, toasted
½ head cabbage, chopped or w small head—chopped
4 green onions, chopped
1 pkg. chicken-flavored noodles, broken up

Combine cabbage, onions and noodles. Reserve sesame seeds and almonds.

For the dressing:
    2 Tbsp. sugar
    ½ cup oil
    3 Tbsp. Vinegar
    ½ tsp. salt
    1 pkg. flavor from noodles
    ¼ tsp. pepper

Combine dressing ingredients and put on, along with the almonds and seeds just prior to serving.

* * *

RASPBERRY ANGEL LOAF

Alma Fehrs Corbin—Deceased

1 pkg. raspberry Jell-O
1½ cup boiling water
1 pkg. frozen or fresh raspberries
1 cup whipping cream, or substitute Cool Whip instead
1 prepared angel food cake
A dash of salt

Break cake into bite sizes and set aside. Mix Jell-O in boiling water and add raspberries and salt—refrigerate until slightly set. Whip cream until soft peaks appear—fold into Jell-O mixture.

In an angel food cake pan, scatter about one fourth of cake pieces in bottom—pour about one fourth of Jell-O mixture over the pieces—then add the rest of the cake pieces and Jell-O mixture in alternating one fourth layers. Refrigerate until set—then remove from pan onto a cake platter.

Store in refrigerator until served.

* * *

READY HAMBURGER MIX

Jean Bruinier Nash—Deceased

4 lbs. lean ground beef
1 large onion, chopped
2 tsp. salt
½ tsp. pepper
½ tsp. oregano
¼ tsp. garlic salt

Brown ground beef in a heavy skillet. Drain. Add onion and continue cooking over medium-low heat until onions are golden. Add remaining ingredients. Cool. Spoon mixture into four 1-pint freezer containers, leaving ½ inch space at top. Seal and label containers. Freeze
Use within 3 months. Makes about 4 pints.

* * *

RECIPE FOR A MARRIAGE

Ruth Corbin Graves—Deceased

Ingredients:

Love	Patience
Humor	Companionship
Trust	Tenderness

Blend ingredients together, add joy, and sprinkle with kisses.

Serve.

* * *

RECIPE FOR PRESERVING CHILDREN

Ruth Corbin Graves—Deceased

Take one grassy field, ½ dozen children. 2 small dogs, a small brook, and some pebbles.

Mix the children and dogs together and put them in the field, stirring constantly. Pour the brook over the pebbles, Sprinkle the field with flowers. Spread over all a deep blue sky and bake in the hot sun. When brown, remove and set away to cool in a bathtub.

*   *   *

RECIPE TO PRESERVE A HUSBAND

Ruth Corbin Graves—Deceased

In choosing a husband, women should first be careful of their selection. Do not choose too young or too green, and take only such as have been raised in a good moral atmosphere. When you have decided on your selection, turn your thoughts to domestic use. Some wives insist on keeping husbands in a pickle, while others constantly are getting them in hot water. This will only make them sour, hard, and sometimes bitter. Even the poorest varieties can be made sweet, tender, and good by garnishing them with patience, spicing them with smiles, and flavoring them with kisses. For a finished product, husbands should be wrapped in a mantle of kindness, kept warm with the fire of devotion, and served with peaches and cream. Husbands prepared this way will keep for years.

*   *   *

RELISH

Alma Fehrs Corbin—Deceased

8 large cucumbers, either green or ripe

Peel, remove seeds, and dice. Salt lightly and let stand overnight.

In the morning, drain and add the following, diced:

1 bunch celery
3 green peppers
3 red peppers
2 large onions

Pour over 4 cups vinegar and 5 cups sugar. Add 2 Tbsp. white mustard seed. Cook all together until vegetables look clear.

Do not overcook. Seal hot. Yields 5 pints.

*   *   *

RHUBARB PIE

Alma Fehrs Corbin—Deceased

2 cups rhubarb cut in small pieces
1 cup sugar
1 tsp. butter
1 egg
4 tsp. flour
1 tsp. cinnamon

In mixing bowl, beat egg, add flour, sugar and cinnamon. Pour rhubarb on mixture and stir until all pieces are coated.

Pour into pie shell, dot with butter, add top crust, and bake in moderate oven {about 265 degrees} for 45 minutes

The rhubarb was picked from her own garden.

*   *   *

ROUND POPPY SEED LOAVES

Peggy Ann Corbin—Deceased

1 pkg. dry yeast
1 cup warm water
Sugar
½ cup oil
1 tsp. salt
2 eggs
2 Tbsp. poppy seeds
4½ to 5 cups flour
Some parchment paper
3 to 4 empty coffee cans

Combine yeast, ½ cup warm water and a dash of sugar. Let stand 5 minutes until bubbly and light. In large mixing bowl, combine remaining ½ cup warm water, ¼ cup sugar, oil, salt and yeast mixture and blend well. Blend in eggs and poppy seeds. Add flour, 1 cup at a time, blending well after each addition until dough is soft. Sprinkle flour on pastry board and turn dough out onto flour. Knead flour into dough, folding and punching until smooth and satiny, usually about 5 minutes.

Place dough in greased bowl, turning to coat. Cover with towel and let rise in warm place until doubled, usually about an hour. Then Knead dough and divide to fill ¼ to ⅓ of 4 well-greased 1 lb. (or 3 2-lb.) coffee cans lined with parchment paper circles on bottom. Cover with towel and let rise in warm place until doubled, about 45 minutes. Place cans on baking sheet and bake at 375 degrees for 30 to 35 minutes or until tops are golden brown. Carefully remove from cans. If bread is difficult to remove, loosen with sharp knife or take off bottom with a can opener and gently push bread out. Return loaves to oven on baking sheet and bake an additional 5 to 10 minutes or until golden brown.

*   *   *

SALTED PEANUT COOKIES

Linda Kirk Pierce—Deceased

1 cup brown sugar
2 eggs
1 cu p white sugar
1½ cups salted peanuts
¾ cup butter
1 tsp. soda
3 cups oatmeal
1½ cups flour
1 tsp. vanilla
1 tsp. baking powder

Cream sugars and butter. Add eggs, beating well, and vanilla.

Mix together flour, soda and baking powder and add to mixture.

Stir in oatmeal and peanuts. Drop by rounded spoonful {about a tsp.} onto cookie sheet.

Bake at 350 degrees until brown

* * *

SAUERKRAUT SALAD { Relish }

Catherin Nash Bosmoe—Deceased

1 #2½ can kraut
1 cup white sugar
1 small green pepper, chopped
1 onion, chopped
½ to 1 tsp. celery seed
1 can pimento

Mix and let set overnight

*   *   *

SCALLOPED CORN

Ruth Corbin Graves—Deceased

2 cans corn
1 cup milk
2 eggs, beaten
1 cup (approx.) soda crackers, broken and crushed

Bake in medium oven for 20 to 25 minutes. Bacon and cheese may be placed on top of the corn mixture for a different flavor.

* * *

SCALLOPED POTATOES WITH MUSHROOM SOUP

Alma Fehrs Corbin-Deceased

8 medium potatoes, sliced
¼ cup diced onion
¼ cup diced green pepper
1 can mushroom soup
¾ cup milk
2 tsp. salt
Dash of pepper

Arrange potatoes, onions, and green peppers in alternating layers. Combine other ingredients and pour over everything in a glass baking dish. Bake for 1 hour at 375 degrees.

* * *

SEVEN-UP SALAD

Lulu Corbin Nash—Deceased

Dissolve in 3 cups boiling water:
    1 pkg. lime Jell-O
    2 3-oz.pkgs. lemon Jell-O

Combine with:
    3 cups of 7-Up
    1 cup marshmallows, small
    3 bananas, mashed
    1 can crushed pineapple, drained

For the Topping, combine:
    1 cup pineapple juice or 7-Up
    1 egg
    2 Tbsp. flour
    ½ cup sugar

Cook until thick. Cool. Add 1 cup whipped cream.
Spread on salad when set.

*   *   *

SIMPLIFIED QUICHE

Jean Bruinier Nash—Deceased

1 egg, separated
1 baked pie crust, flaky pie crust
4 strips bacon, partially cooked, chopped
1 ¾ cups milk or cream
1 cup grated Swiss cheese
¼ tsp. paprika or tsp. minced onion
Dash of cayenne pepper
3 eggs
Chicken gravy, if desired
Pimento, for garnish
½ tsp. salt

Beat egg white and brush on bottom of pie crust. Reserve egg yolk. Sprinkle bacon evenly over bottom of crust. Scald milk or cream in a medium saucepan. Reduce heat and add grated cheese. Stir until cheese is melted. Add salt, paprika, onion and cayenne pepper. Remove from heat and cool slightly. Add 3 eggs plus reserved yolk 1 at a time, beating well after each. Pour into pie crust. Bake about 45 minutes, until toothpick inserted in center comes out clean. Serve with chicken gravy, if desired. Garnish with pimiento. Makes 1 quiche.

* * *

SLOPPY JOE'S FOR A CROWD

Delores Storly Corbin—Deceased

Brown:
   10 lbs. ground beef
   5 large onions, minced

Add:
   3 cups catsup
   ½ cup Worcestershire sauce
   ½ cup steak sauce
   2½ tsp. chili powder
   1 tsp. celery salt
   Salt and pepper to taste
   Tomato juice for consistency

Fry until meat is brown, stirring occasionally to keep everything separated. Then using whatever kind of bun you like to eat, spread a layer of this concoction about a quarter inch deep, then eat and enjoy.

* * *

SNOW ON THE MOUNTAIN BUFFET DINNER

Olive Brice Grace—Deceased

1) Base for a mountain, make it broad
   4 cups of dry rice, cooked

2) Main course, don't short yourself
   2 chickens stewed in broth, deboned and thickened

3) Right in the middle of the pile
   5 cups fresh tomatoes, cut up

4) Scatter a little for flavor
   green onions, chopped

5) Don't be backward—Chinese noodles
   2 large cans dry noodles

6) For a crispier
   1 bunch of celery, cut up

7) For more flavor
   2 large cans olives, sliced. (1 ripe and 1 green stuffed)

8) Essential too
   2 cups shredded cheese

9) Unusually Delicious
   1 large can crushed pineapple, drained

10) The Oriental Touch
    1 large bag of slivered almonds

11) The Snow
    1 large bag of flaked coconuts

Arrange buffet style with signs, may serve rolls and dessert.
Serves 10.

*   *   *

SOFT BUNS

Alma Fehrs Corbin—Deceased

Dissolve 2 pkgs, yeast in ½ cup warm water.
Mix together 2 cups of warm milk
½ cup sugar
⅓ cup shortening, melted
2 eggs, beaten
1 Tbsp. salt

Stir in the yeast mixture, adding enough flour to make a soft dough. Let rise, kneed down and let rise again. Make out into rolls or buns.

Bake in moderate oven until rolls or buns are brown on top.

* * *

SOUR CREAM CHOCOLATE CAKE

Delores Storly Corbin—Deceased

2 rounded Tbsp. butter or margarine
2 cups sugar
2 eggs, beaten
½ cup cocoa, sifted
2 tsp. soda
1 cup sour cream
2½ cups flour, sifted
1 cup cold water

Cream butter, margarine and sugar. Add the cocoa, and 2 eggs. Combine sour cream and soda and add to cake mixture alternately with sifted flour. Add 1 cup cold water last.
Bake at 350 degrees for 30 to 35 minutes.

*   *   *

SOUR CREAM PEACH PIE

Alma Fehrs Corbin—Deceased

In 1 unbaked pie shell, Sprinkle in bottom of shell:
2 Tbsp. flour,
2 Tbsp. tapioca and ½ cup white sugar

Slice 4 to 5 peaches on this. Mix 1 cup sour cream, and 1 cup of brown sugar—pour over peaches and sprinkle with cinnamon.
Bake for 1 hour at 375 degrees.

* * *

SOUR CREAM RAISIN PIE

Alma Fehrs Corbin—Deceased

1 cup sour cream
1 cup raisins
2 eggs, separated {use yolks in filling}
⅔ cup sugar
Dash of cinnamon and orange peel, grated
A pinch of salt

Beat egg yolks and sugar together, add sour cream, raisins and spice. Pour into pastry-lined pie pan and bake as a custard pie for ten minutes at 450 degrees— then lower temperature to 300 degrees until firm. When done, remove from oven. Beat egg whites until thick and glossy, adding 4 Tbsp. sugar and a dash of salt.

Spread meringue on pie and bake at 375 degrees or until lightly browned.

* * *

SPAGHETTI AND MEAT BALLS

Alma Fehrs Corbin—Deceased

1 onion, chopped
3 Tbsp. fat
1 cup water
½ tsp. pepper
1 bay leaf
½ cup rice, uncooked
2 eggs, well beaten
1 8-oz.pkg. spaghetti, cooked
1 clove garlic, minced
1 qt. tomato juice
1 tsp. salt
1 Tbsp. sugar
1 lb. ground beef
½ cup milk
Salt and pepper

Brown onion and garlic in hot fat. Add tomato juice, water and seasonings. Cook slowly on hour. Cook rice and add to ground beef, eggs, milk and salt and pepper. Form into small balls and brown in hot fat. Add these to the sauce and simmer for 15 minutes. Either add spaghetti or pour over the spaghetti. Serves 6 to 8.

* * *

SPAGHETTI PIE

Peggy Ann Corbin—Deceased

6 oz. spaghetti
⅓ cup grated parmesan cheese
1 lb. ground beef or bulk pork sausage
½ cup chopped onion
¼ cup chopped green pepper
1 8-oz. can tomatoes, cut up
½ cup shredded mozzarella cheese (2 oz)
2 Tbsp. butter or margarine
2 well-beaten eggs
1 cup (8 oz) cottage cheese
1 6 oz. can tomato paste
1 tsp. sugar
½ tsp. garlic salt
1 tsp. dried oregano, crushed

Cook the spaghetti according to package directions, drain (should have about 3 cups of spaghetti). Stir butter or margarine into hot spaghetti. Stir in Parmesan cheese and eggs. Form spaghetti mixture into a "crust" in a buttered 10-inch pie plate. Spread cottage cheese over bottom of spaghetti crust. In skillet cook ground beef or pork sausage, onion, and green pepper until vegetables are tender and meat is browned. Drain off excess fat. Stir in undrained tomatoes, tomato paste, sugar, oregano, and garlic salt, heat through. Turn meat mixture into spaghetti crust.

Bake uncovered, in 350 degree oven for 20 minutes. Sprinkle the mozzarella cheese atop. Bake another 5 minutes longer until cheese melts.

Makes six servings. This is very good eating.

* * *

SPARE RIBS AND BARBECUE SAUCE

Olive Brice Grace—Deceased

This recipe was obtained from a cook at a Portland, Oregon fire station.

2 spare ribs
½ cup chopped onion
1 cup catsup
3 Tbsp. brown sugar
1 cup water
2 tsp. dry mustard
½ cup vinegar
1 tsp. salt
1 Tbsp. Worcestershire sauce
¼ tsp. pepper

Combine ingredients and pour over spare ribs. Bake 2 to 3 hours at 350 degrees.

* * *

SPINACH SALAD

Olive Brice Grace—Deceased

3 bunches spinach, washed and dried
1 cup shredded cheese
1 cup bean sprouts
1 cup crumbled cooked bacon

Dressing:
    ½ cup sugar
    1 cup oil
    ⅔ cup catsup
    ¼ cup brown vinegar
    Salt and pepper to taste
    2 Tbsp. Worcestershire sauce

Mix all of the salad makings together in a bowl made from glass or metal.

Then after mixing all of the dressing ingredients together, gently mix with the Salad makings. Enjoy.

*   *   *

STEAMED CARROT PUDDING

Lyle Corbin Pierce—Deceased

This was a recipe of my mother—Verdie Fisk Corbin

1 cup grated carrots
½ tsp. of each, cinnamon, cloves, and nutmeg
1 cup grated raw potatoes
1 cup sugar
1 cup flour {heaping}
About ½ tsp. salt
1 cup chopped suet
½ cup raisins
½ cup currants

Stir 1 tsp. soda into potatoes and mix thoroughly all ingredients.

Steam 3 hours. Two cups of bread crumbs is a great improvement

* * *

STRAWBERRY JAM

Alma Fehrs Corbin—Deceased

To 1 qt. of strawberries, add 3 Tbsp. vinegar and bring to full rolling boil. Continue boiling for 3 minutes, add 4 cups sugar and again bring to full rolling boil. Continue to boil for ten minutes, skive.

Let stand overnight in enamel kettle. Seal when cold.

* * *

STRAWBERRY SALAD

Catherin Nash Bosmoe—Deceased

2 3-oz.pkgs, strawberry Jell-O
2 cups hot water
1 pt. frozen strawberries and juice
1 tall can crushed pineapple and juice
2 mashed bananas

Mix all ingredients together.
Divide and put ½ of mixture in 9 by 13 inch pan.
When almost set, spread pint of sour cream over surface and pour in remaining strawberry mixture as the third layer.
Chill for at least 2 hours.

* * *

SUPER SALAD SEASONING MIX

Jean Bruinier Nash—Deceased

2 cups grated parmesan cheese
½ tsp. dried dill seed
2 tsp. salt
2 Tbsp. poppy seeds
1 tsp. monosodium glutamate—if desired
½ cup sesame seeds
½ tsp, garlic salt
1 Tbsp. instant minced onion
3 Tbsp. celery seeds
2 tsp. paprika
2 Tbsp. parsley flakes
½ tsp. fresh ground pepper

Combine all ingredients in a small bowl. Mix until evenly distributed. Put in a 1 qt. airtight container. Label the container.

Store in a cool, dry place. Use within 3 to 4 months.

Makes about 3 cups.

* * *

SUPER STRENGTH CHICKEN STOCK

Peggy Chapman Corbin—Deceased

4 lbs chicken pieces: back, neck, wings, heart, gizzard, etc.
2 yellow onions, unpeeled
1 leek, cleaned and chopped
2 carrots, peeled and roughly chopped
2 stalks celery with leaves chopped also
2 turnips, peeled and roughly chopped
2 parsnips, peeled and roughly chopped
1 tsp. chopped fresh thyme or ½ tsp. dried thyme
4 quarts filtered water
2 cloves garlic
8 sprigs parsley
4 whole cloves
10 peppercorns
1 tsp. salt
1 small bay leaf
2 Tbsp. red-wine vinegar

Place chicken pieces in large pot and add enough water to cover chicken totally. Heat to boiling. Boil 5 minutes, skimming surface to remove scum. Add onions, leek, garlic, carrots, celery, turnips, parsnips, parsley, cloves, peppercorn, salt, bay leaf, thyme, and vinegar with enough water to cover chicken by 3 inches. Return to boiling, then reduce heat to low. Simmer, partially covered, skimming surface occasionally, until stock is reduced to 1½ quarts, probably about 3 hours. Strain.
Makes 1½ quarts.

* * *

SWEET AND SOUR SPARERIBS

Neva Martin Hazen Ruth—Deceased

2 lbs. spareribs, lean as possible
½ cup brown sugar
1 large can pineapple juice
⅛ cup vinegar
1 large onion, chopped
3 Tbsp. corn starch
1 green pepper, chopped
3 Tbsp. soy sauce
2 Tbsp. water

Brown ribs and onion. Add pineapple juice, cover and cook for 40 minutes. Add green peppers. Mix remaining ingredients and add to rib mixture. Cook until thick. Serve over rice.

*   *   *

TACO SALAD

Linda Kirk Pierce—Deceased

1 head lettuce, broken up
1 cup cheese, shredded
2 tomatoes, cut up
1 lb. hamburger
1 pkg. corn chips
½ of 8-oz. bottle of mild taco sauce
      or
1 pkg. taco seasoning and 1 can tomato sauce

Brown hamburger, add taco sauce. Place lettuce in salad bowl—add cheese and tomatoes.

When ready to serve, add hamburger mixture to lettuce, toss—then add ½ of corn chips and toss again.

Serve rest of corn chips on the side.

* * *

TEXAS BROWNIES

Linda Kirk Pierce—Deceased

2 cups flour
¼ cup dark unsweetened cocoa
2 cups sugar
½ cup butter or margarine
½ cup buttermilk
2 eggs
½ cup shortening
1 tsp. baking soda
1 tsp. vanilla
1 cup strong brewed coffee

In a large mixing bowl, combine flour and sugar, set aside.

In a heavy sauce pan, combine butter, shortening, coffee and cocoa

Place over heat and bring to boil, keeping it stirred.

Pour boiling mixture over the flour and sugar.

Add buttermilk, egg, baking soda and vanilla. Mix well.

Pour into a well-buttered 17½ by 11 inch jelly roll pan.

Bake at 400 degrees for twenty minutes.

While brownies bake, make the frosting.

Recipe for the frosting:
    ½ cup butter or margarine
    ½ cup milk
    2 tsp. dark cocoa
    1 tsp. vanilla
    3½ cups powdered sugar

In a sauce pan, combine butter, cocoa and milk—heat to boiling, stirring constantly. Add powdered sugar and vanilla—beat until smooth.

Pour warm frosting over brownies as soon as you remove pan from oven. Let them cool for a while, then cut into 48 brownies.

* * *

THREE LAYER DESSERT

Linda Kirk Pierce—Deceased

1st Layer {crust}:

Melt ½ cup margarine in 9 by 13 inch cake pan.
Add 1 cup flour and 1 cup nuts.
Bake 15 minutes at 350 degrees then let cool when done.

2nd Layer:

1 cup powdered sugar and 1 8-oz. cream cheese.
Mix together and add 2 cups Cool Whip. Spread on cooled crust.

3rd Layer:

2 pkgs. instant pudding and 3 cups milk.
Beat and pour mixture on top. Refrigerate.
Top with Cool Whip just before serving

* * *

24-HOUR SALAD

Linda Kirk Pierce—Deceased

Create layers in a 13 by 9 by 2 inch dish in order listed:

1 head of lettuce, shredded
4 stalks of celery, sliced thin
1 small red onion, sliced thin
1 pkg. frozen peas, uncooked, rinsed and drained
1 can of water chestnuts, drained and sliced
1 green pepper, chopped

Cover with 2 cups mayonnaise mixed with 2 Tbsp. sugar.
Sprinkle liberally with Parmesan cheese {Shredded cheddar can also be used}. Cover with Saran Wrap. Refrigerate overnight.

Before serving, sprinkle with bacon bits from $1/3$ lb. crisp-fried bacon. Garnish over top with 4 hard-boiled eggs, sliced.

* * *

TWO TONED DESSERT

Vivian Corbin Brice—Deceased

Bottom Crust:
Mix like pastry and pat into bottom of a 9 by 13 inch pan.
Assemble:
    1 cube margarine
    1 cup flour
    ½ cup chopped walnuts
Bake 12 to 15 minutes at 350 degrees—then let it cool.

2nd Layer:
    1 8-oz. pkg. cream cheese, softened
Beat in mixer and slowly add 1 cup sifted powdered sugar until light and fluffy
Mix in ½ container of Cool Whip
Spread on 1st layer and set.

3rd Layer:
    1 large pkg. chocolate Jell-O instant pudding,
    2 ½ cups cold milk.
Mix according to directions on pkg.
Spread on 2nd layer.

4th Layer:
Spread remainder of Cool Whip over 3rd layer.

5th Layer:
Top with 1 cup toasted coconut.

Refrigerate 6 to 8 hours, or overnight. Perfect for that "Just right" dessert.

*   *   *

UNBEATEN MARRIAGE

Ruth Corbin Graves—Deceased

1 tender young man
1 freshly picked woman

Bring to slow boil by adding:

2 kisses
Several kind words
1 love pat
2 pairs helping hands
1 head of wisdom
Lots of understanding
1 heaping hand of courage
2 heads of common sense
2 large hearts
Dash of jealousy

Simmer in a large house for years and years

* * *

VEAL CORDON BLEU

Peggy Ann Corbin—Deceased

¾ cup skim milk
1 tsp. lemon juice
¼ tsp. dried tarragon
¼ tsp. white pepper
Salt to taste

Optional:
  ½ tsp. MSG
  1 lb. leanest veal cutlets in 4 serving pieces
  1 tsp. corn oil
  2 lean cooked thin ham slices
  2 thin slices Swiss cheese
  ½ tsp. vanilla extract
  ¼ cup bread crumbs

Mix milk with lemon juice, tarragon, pepper, salt, and MSG. Put aside.

Pound cutlets until double in size and ⅛ inch thick. Cut each in half width-wise, making 8 square cutlets. Place in shallow dish and cover with milk mixture. Cover and refrigerate 6 hours or overnight. Remove cutlets from marinade, reserve marinade. Pat cutlets dry with paper towels. Place 1 cutlet on cutting board. Place ½ slice ham and ½ slice cheese on meat, leaving a ½ inch edge of cutlet uncovered. Moisten edges of veal with a little egg. Top with another cutlet and pound edges with mallet to seal.

Repeat, making 4 cutlets. Mix ½ cup of reserved milk marinade with remaining egg, oil, and vanilla. Spread crumbs in shallow dish. Dip both sides of each filled cutlet, first in milk-egg mixture, then in bread crumbs. Spray non-stick skillet with PAM.

Quickly brown cutlets on each side. Place cutlets in non-stick baking dish. Bake uncovered at 350 degrees for 20 to 25 minutes. This makes four servings. Serve with asparagus and fresh tomato slices.

* * *

VEGETABLE CASSEROLE

Linda Kirk Pierce—Deceased

Melt together:
½ cup American cheese
¼ cup butter.

Add 1 pkg. each: frozen cauliflower, broccoli, carrots, thawed and drained. Place in baking dish.

Mix ¼ cup melted butter with ½ cup crushed crackers and sprinkle over top.

Bake at 350 degrees for 20 to 25 minutes.

* * *

VEGETABLE SALAD

Linda Kirk Pierce—Deceased

This is a quick and easy salad

1 head cauliflower, broken up
2 tomatoes, chopped
1 head broccoli, broken up
1 small red onion
1 cup cheese, shredded or cubed

Mix all ingredients together—then add 1 cup of Miracle Whip

*   *   *

VEGETABLE STOCK

Peggy Chapman Corbin—Deceased

¼ cup unsalted butter
4 stalks celery w/leaves chopped
4 carrots, peeled and roughly chopped
½ oz. dried mushrooms
2 leeks, cleaned and chopped
1 tsp. chopped fresh thyme or ½ tsp. dried thyme
1 fresh sage leaf or dash dried sage
½ tsp. crushed dried hot red chilies
Dash of freshly grated nutmeg
1 Tbsp. red wine vinegar
5 onions, chopped
2 cloves garlic
1 bunch parsley
1 bay leaf
1½ tsp. salt
10 peppercorns, lightly crushed
10 allspice berries, lightly crushed
4 qts. water

Melt butter in large heavy pot over medium heat. Stir in onions. Cook 5 minutes. Add garlic, celery, carrots, leeks, mushrooms, parsley, thyme, sage, bay leaf, salt, peppercorns, allspice, nutmeg, and water. Heat to boiling. Reduce heat to low. Simmer partially covered until reduced to about 2½ qts., about 2 hours. Add chilies and vinegar. Simmer uncovered, 30 minutes longer. Strain, gently pressing liquid out of vegetables with back of spoon. Makes 1 ½ to 2 quarts.

* * *

WALNUT SLICES

Neva Martin Hazen Ruth—Deceased

1 cup flour
½ cup butter

Mix above with hands and press into 8 x 8 inch pan. Bake at 350 degrees in oven for 10 minutes.

Mix together:
1½ cup brown sugar
1 cup chopped nuts
1 Tbsp. flour
2 eggs
½ cup coconut
½ tsp. baking powder

Mix and spread over first mixture. Bake at 320 degrees for 20 minutes.
Cool well. Cut into squares.

* * *

WILD BLACKBERRY COBBLER

Ruth Corbin Graves—Decease

1 quart or more of blackberries
1 cup sugar
a pinch of salt
a dash of cinnamon
3 Tbsp. cornstarch
2 pie crusts

Make your favorite pie crust recipe, enough for a 2 crust pie.

For bottom crust, roll out dough in a rectangular patter for a 9 by 13 inch pan, and place in bottom of pan. In a bowl, mix blackberries, sugar, salt, cinnamon and cornstarch. Pour berries on crust evenly.

Roll out top crust. Cut slits in top crust with knife, place over berries and flute edges if desired. Sprinkle sugar on top crust and bake at medium heat at about 350 degrees in oven until berries bubble and crust is light brown....

This is Delicious....

I used native berries of Southwest Missouri that grow on our farm.

* * *

YELLOW ANGEL FOOD CAKE

Alma Fehrs Corbin—Deceased
"Clarence Corbin's favorite cake"

Sift five times:
1½ cups cake flour
½ tsp. cream of tartar
½ tsp. baking powder

Combine and beat 15 minutes:
10 to 11 eggs yolks
½ cup cold water
pinch of salt

Fold into egg mixture:
1 cup sugar
1 tsp. lemon extract.

Add flour just like angel food cake. Bake at 325 degrees for 1 hour.

* * *

ZUCCHINI SUNSHINE PRESERVE

Lulu Corbin Nash—Deceased

6 cups sugar
6 cups grated zucchini

Combine all above ingredients and boil five minutes
Add one 6 oz. pkg. orange Jell-O
Put in jars and seal.

* * *

PART TWO

BAKING PERFECT DESSERTS

For Perfect Cookies

Cookie dough that is to be rolled is much easier to handle after it has been refrigerated for 10 to 30 minutes. This keeps the dough from sticking, even though it may be soft. If not done, the soft dough may require more flour and too much flour makes cookies hard and brittle. In rolling, take out on a floured board, only as much dough as can be easily managed. Flour the rolling pin slightly and roll lightly to desired thickness. Cut shapes close together and keep all trimmings for the last. Place pans or sheets in upper third of oven. Watch cookies carefully while baking to avoid burning edges. When sprinkling sugar on cookies, try putting it into saltshaker's. It saves time.

* * *

FOR PERFECT PIES AND CAKES

A pie crust will be more easily made and better if all the Ingredients are cool.

The lower crust should be placed in the pan so that it covers the surface smoothly. Be sure no air lurks beneath the surface, for it will push the crust out of shape in baking.

Folding the top crust over the lower crust before crimping will keep the juices in the pie.

In making custard type pies, bake at a high temperature for about ten minutes to prevent a soggy crust. Then finish baking at a low temperature.

Fill cake pans about $^2/_3$ full and spread batter well into corners and to the sides leaving a slight hollow in the center.

The cake is done when it shrinks from the sides of the pan or if it springs back when touched lightly with the finger.

After a cake comes from the oven, it should be placed on a rack for about five minutes. Then the sides should be loosened and the cake turned out on a rack to finish cooling.

Cakes should not be frosted until thoroughly cool.

To prevent crust from becoming soggy with cream pie, sprinkle crust with powdered sugar.

*   *   *

TEMPERATURE CHART

FOOD	TEMPERATURE	TIME
Butter cake, Loaf	380—400	40-60 min
Butter cake, layer	380—400	20-40 min
Cake, angel	300—360	50-60 min
Cake, sponge	300—350	40-60 min
Cake, fruit	275—325	3-4 hours
Cookies, thin	380—390	10-15 min
Cookies, molasses	350—375	18-20 min
Cream puffs	300—350	45-60 min
Meringue	250—300	40-60 min
Pie Crust	400—500	20-40 min

* * *

BAKING PERFECT BREADS

PROPORTIONS

Biscuits   to 1 cup flour use 1¼ teas. baking powder

Muffins   to 1 cup flour use 1½ teas. baking powder

Popovers   to 1 cup flour use 1¼ teas. baking powder

Waffles   to 1 cup flour use 1¼ teas. baking powder

Cake w/ oil   to 1 cup flour use 1 teaspoon baking powder

*   *   *

RULES FOR USE OF LEAVENING AGENTS

To 1 teaspoon soda use 2¼ teaspoons cream of tartar, or 2 cups freshly soured milk, or 1 cup molasses.

In simple flour mixtures, use 2 teaspoons baking powder to leaven 1 cup flour. Reduce this amount ½ teaspoon for each egg used.

To substitute soda and an acid for baking powder, divide the amount of baking powder by 4. Take that as your measure of and add the acid according to rule 1 above.

*   *   *

PROPORTIONS FOR BATTERS AND DOUGH

Pour Batter   to 1 cup liquid, use 1 cup flour

Drop Batter   to 1 cup liquid, use 2 to 2½ cups flour

Soft Dough   to 1 cup liquid, use 3 to 3½ cups flour

Stiff Dough   to 1 cup liquid, use 4 cups flour

*   *   *

TIPS FOR BAKING BREADS

Kneading the dough for a half minute after mixing the texture of baking powder biscuits.

Use cooking or salad oil in waffles and hot cakes in the place of shortening. Use extra pan or bowl to melt the shortening and no waiting.

When bread is baking, a small dish of water in the oven will help to keep the crust from getting hard.

Dip the spoon in hot water to measure shortening butter, etc. the fat will slip out more easily.

Small amounts of leftover corn may be added to pancake batter for variety.

To make bread crumbs, use fine cutter of the food grinder and tie a large paper bag over the spout to prevent flying crumbs.

When you are doing any sort of baking, you get better results if you remember to pre-heat your cookie sheet, muffin tins, or cake pans.

* * *

OVEN TEMPERATURE CHART

BREADS	MINUTES	TEMPERATURE
Loaf	50-60	350-400
Rolls	20-30	400-450
Biscuits	12-15	400-450
Popovers	30-40	425-450
Cornbread	25-30	400-425
Nut Breads	50-75	350
Gingerbread	40-50	350-370

* * *

MEASUREMENTS & SUBSTITUTIONS

For liquid and dry measurements use standard measuring spoons and cups. All measurements are level.

Measurements	Substitutions
a pinch	$1/8$ teaspoon or less
3 teaspoons	1 tablespoon
4 tablespoons	$1/4$ cup
8 tablespoons	$1/2$ cup
12 tablespoons	$3/4$ cup
16 tablespoons	1 cup
2 cups	1 pint
4 cups	1 quart
4 quarts	1 gallon
8 quarts	1 peck
4 pecks	1 bushel
16 ounces	1 pound
32 ounces	1 quart
8 ounces liquid	1 cup
1 ounce of liquid	2 tablespoons

* * *

MEASUREMENTS AND SUBSTITUTIONS

INGREDIENTS, QUANTITY, SUBSTITUTES

Self-rising flour, 1 cup, substitute:
   1 cup all-purpose flour, ½ tsp. salt & 1 tsp. baking powder

Cornstarch, 1 tablespoon, substitute:
   2 tbsp. flour
   or 2 tsp. of cooking tapioca

Baking powder, 1 teaspoon, substitute:
   ¼ tsp. baking soda plus ½ tsp. cream of tarter

Powdered sugar, 1 cup, substitute:
   1 cup granulated sugar plus 1 tsp. cornstarch

Brown sugar, ½ cup, substitute:
   2 tbsp. molasses in ½ cup of granulated sugar

Sour milk, 1 cup, substitute:
   1 tbsp. lemon juice or vinegar, plus sweet milk to make 1 cup, let stand 5 minutes

Whole milk, 1 cup, substitute;
   ½ cup evaporated milk plus ½ cup of water

Fresh herbs, 1 Tbsp., substitute:
   1 tsp. dried herbs

Fresh onions, 1 small, substitute:
   1 tbsp. instant minced onion, rehydrated

Dry mustard, 1tsp., substitute:
  1 Tbsp. prepared mustard

Tomato juice, 1 cup, substitute:
  ½ cup tomato sauce, plus ½ cup water

Catsup or chili sauce, 1 cup, substitute:
  1 cup tomato sauce plus ½ cup sugar and 2 Tbsp. vinegar
  (or use in cooking)

Dates, 1 lb., substitute:
  1½ cup dates, pitted and cut open

Bananas, 3 medium, substitute:
  1 cup mashed

Miniature marshmallows, 10, substitute:
  1 large marshmallow

In substituting cocoa for chocolate in cakes, the amount of flour must be reduced.

Brown and white sugars may usually be used interchangeably.

* * *

TERMS USED IN COOKING

AU GRATIN: topped with crumbs and or cheese and browned in the oven or under broiler.

AU JUS: served in its own juices.

BASTE: to moisten foods during cooking with pan drippings or special sauce to add flavor and prevent drying.

BISQUE: a thick cream soup

BLANCH: to immerse in rapidly boiling water and allow to cook, slightly.

CREAM: to soften a fat. especially butter, by beating it at room temperature. Butter and sugar are often creamed together, making a smooth, soft paste.

CRIMP: to seal the edges of a two crust pie either by pinching them at intervals with the fingers or by pressing them together with the tines of a fork.

CRUDITÉS: an assortment of raw vegetables, that is, carrots, broccoli, mushrooms, served as an hors d' oeuvre often accompanied by a dip.

DEGREASE: to remove fat from the surface of stews, soups, or stock. Usually cooled in the refrigerator, so that fat hardens and is easily removed.

DREDGE: to coat lightly with flour, cornmeal, etc.

ENTRÉE: the main course.

FOLD: to incorporate a delicate substance, such as whipped cream or beaten egg whites, into another substance without releasing air bubbles. A spatula is used to gently bring part of the mixture from the bottom of the bowl to the top. The process is repeated, while slowly rotating the bowl, until the ingredients are thoroughly blended.

GLAZE: to cover with a glossy coating such as melted and somewhat diluted jelly for fruit desserts.

JULIENNE: to cut vegetables, fruits, or cheeses into match shaped slivers.

MARIANADE: to allow food to stand in a liquid to tenderize or to add flavor.

MEUNIERE: dredged with flour and sautéed in butter

MINCE: to chop or cut food into very small pieces.

PARBOIL: to boil until partially cooked, to blanch. Usually final cooking in a seasoned sauce follows this procedure.

PARE: to remove the outermost skin of a fruit or vegetable.

POUCH: to cook very gently in hot liquid kept just below the boiling point.

PUREE: to mash foods until perfectly smooth by hand, by rubbing through a sieve or food mill, or by whirling in a blender or food processor.

REFRESH: to run cold water over food that has been par-boiled, to stop the cooking process quickly.

SAUTE: to cook and or brown food in a small quantity of hot shortening.

SCALD: to heat to just below the boiling point, when tiny bubbles appear at the edge of the saucepan.

SIMMER: to cook in liquid just below the boiling point. The surface of the liquid should be barely moving, broken from time to time by slowly rising bubbles.

STEEP: to let food stand in (hot) liquid to extract or to enhance flavor, like tea in hot water or poached fruits in sugar syrup.

TOSS: to combine ingredients with a lifting motion

WHIP: to beat rapidly to incorporate air and produce expansion, as in heavy cream or egg whites.

*   *   *

COOKING TIPS

After stewing a chicken for diced meat for casseroles, etc. let cool in broth before cutting into chunks—it will have twice the flavor.

To slice meat into thin strips, as for Chinese dishes— partially freeze and it will slice easily.

A roast with the bone in will cook faster than a boneless roast—the bone carries the heat to the inside of the roast quicker.

Never cook a roast cold—let stand for at least an hour at room temperature. Brush with oil before and during roast- ing—the oil will seal in the juices.

When roasting any kind of bird (chicken or turkey, duck or pheasant) After stuffing bird with whatever kind of dress- ing you have made. take a brown paper grocery bag and cut one side(wide side) of bag off (throw away) and rub the rest of this bag with butter on the inside of this bag, everywhere. Place this bag over roasting pan and bird. Bake for correct amount of time for whatever bird you are cooking to thor- oughly cook all the way through entire bird. The bag will automatically baste the bird. Make sure the sides of this bag are inside of roasting pan.

For a juicier hamburger add cold water to the beef before grilling ($\frac{1}{2}$ cup to 1 pound of meat).

To freeze meatballs, place them on a cookie sheet until frozen. Place in plastic bags and they will stay separated so that you may remove as many as you want.

To keep cauliflower white while cooking—add a little milk to the water.

When boiling corn, add sugar to the water instead of salt. Salt will toughen the corn.

To ripen tomatoes—put them in a brown paper bag in a dark pantry and they will ripen overnight.

Do not use soda to keep vegetables green. It destroys vitamin C.

When cooking cabbage, place a small tin cup or can half full of vinegar on the stove near the cabbage. It will absorb all of the odor from the cabbage.

Potatoes soaked in salt water for 20 minutes before baking will bake more rapidly.

Let raw potatoes stand in cold water for at least half an hour before frying to improve the crispness of French fried potatoes.

Use greased muffin tins as molds when baking stuffed green Peppers.

A few drops of lemon juice in water will whiten boiled potatoes.

Buy mushrooms before they "open". When stems and caps are attached snugly, mushrooms are truly fresh.

Do not use metal bowls when mixing salads. Use wooden, glass or china.

Lettuce keeps better if you store in refrigerator without washing first so that the leaves are dry. Wash the day you are going to use.

To keep celery crisp—stand it up in a pitcher of cold, salted water and refrigerate.

Don't despair if you've over salted the gravy. Stir in some instant mashed potatoes and you'll repair the damage. Just add a little more liquid to offset the thickening.

EQUIVALENCY CHART

FOOD	QUANITY	YIELD
Un-sifted flour	3¾ cups	1 pound
Sifted flour	4 cups	1 pound
Sifted cake flour	4½ cups	1 pound
Rye flour	5 cups	1 pound
Flour	1 pound	4 cups
Baking powder	5½ ounces	1 cup
Cornmeal	3 cups	1 pound
Cornstarch	3 cups	1 pound
Lemon	1 medium	3 Tbls. juice
Apple	1 medium	1 cup
Orange	3-4 medium	1 cup juice
Onion	1 medium	½ cup
Unshelled walnuts	1 pound	1½ - 1¾ cups
Sugar	2 cups	1 pound
Powdered sugar	3½ cups	1 pound
Brown sugar	2½ cups	1 pound
Spaghetti	7 ounces	4 cups cooked
Noodles (uncooked)	4 ozs. (1½ cups)	2-3 cups cookd
Macaroni	4 ozs. (1¼ cups)	2¼ cups cookd
Macaroni (cooked)_	6 cups	8 ounce pkg.
Noodles (cooked)	7 cups	8 ounce pkg.
Long-grain rice (unckd)	1 cup	3-4 cups cookd
Saltine crackers	28 crackers	1 cup fine crmbs
Butter	1 stick or ¼ lb.	½ cup
Cocoa	4 cups	1 pound
Chocolate-bitter	1 ounce	1 square
Coconut	2⅔ cups	1½ lb. carton
Marshmallows	16	¼ pound
Graham crackers	14 squares	1 cup fine crmb
Vanilla wafers	22	1 cup fine crmb

Bread	1½ slices	1-cup soft crumbs
Bread	1-slice	¼ cup fine dry crmbs
Egg whites	8-10	1 cup
Egg yolks	10-12	1 cup
Egg	4-5 whole	1 cup
Flavored gelatin	3¼ ounces	½ cup
Unflavored gelatin	¼ ounce	1 tablespoon
Nuts (chopped)	1 cup	¼ pound
Almonds	3½ cups	1 pound
Walnuts (broken)	3 cups	1 pound
Raisins	1 pound	3½ cups
Rice	2⅓ cups	1 pound
American cheese (grated)	5 cups	1 pound
American cheese (cubed)	2⅔ cups	1 pound
Cream cheese	6⅔ Tbls.	3-oz. package
Zwieback (crumbled)	4	1 cup
Banana (mashed)	1 medium	1/3 cup
Coffee (ground)	5 cups	1 pound
Evaporated milk	1 cup	3 cups whipped

* * *

BUYING GUIDE
Fresh Vegetables and Fruits

Experience is the best teacher in choosing quality, but here are a few pointers on buying some of the fruits and vegetables

Asparagus—Stalks should be tender and firm, tips should be close and compact. Choose the stalks with very little white—they are more tender. Use asparagus soon—it toughens rapidly.

Beans, Snap—Those with small seeds inside the pods are best. Avoid beans with dry-looking pods.

Berries—Select plump, solid berries with good color. Avoid stained containers, indicating wet or leaky berries. Berries such as blackberries and raspberries with clinging caps may be under-ripe. Strawberries without caps may be too ripe.

Broccoli, Brussel Sprouts, and Cauliflower—Flower clusters on broccoli and cauliflower should be tight and close together. Brussel sprouts should be firm and compact. Smudgy, dirty spots may indicate insects.

Cabbage and Head Lettuce—Choose heads heavy for size. Avoid cabbage with worm holes, lettuce with discoloration or soft rot.

Cucumbers—Choose long, slender cucumbers for best quality. May be dark or medium green but yellowed once are undesirable.

Melons—In Cantaloupes, thick close netting on the rind indicates best quality. Cantaloupes are ripe when the stem is smooth and space between the netting is yellow or yellow-green. They are best when fully ripe with fruity odor.

Honeydews are ripe when rind has a creamy to yellowish color and velvety texture. Immature honeydews are whitish-green.

Ripe Watermelons have some yellow on one side. If melons are white or pale green on one side, they are not ripe.

Oranges, Grapefruit, and Lemons—Choose those heavy for their size. Smoother, thinner skins usually indicate more juice. Most skin markings do not affect quality. Oranges with a slight greenish tinge may be just as ripe as fully colored ones. Light or greenish-yellow lemons are more tart than deep yellow ones. Avoid citrus fruits showing withered, sunken, or soft areas.

Peas and Lima Beans—Select pods that are well filled but not bulging. Avoid dried spotted, yellowed, or flabby pods.

* * *

TABLE FOR DRIED FRUITS

Fruit	Cooking time	Amt. of Sugar / Honey
Apricots	about 40 minutes	¼ cup per cup of fruit
Figs	about 30 minutes	1 Tbls. per cup of fruit
Peaches	about 45 minutes	¼ cup per cup of fruit
Prunes	about 45 minutes	2 Tbls. per cup of fruit

* * *

MICROWAVE TIPS

Place an open box of hardened brown sugar in the microwave oven with 1 cup of hot water. Microwave at high for 1 ½ to 2 minutes for ½ pound or 2 to 3 minutes for 1 pound.

Soften hard ice cream by micro waving at 30% power. One pint will take 15 to 30 seconds, one quart will take 30 to 45 seconds, and one-half gallon will take 45 to 60 seconds.

One stick of butter or margarine will soften in 1 minute when microwaved at 20% power.

Soften one 8-ounce package of cream cheese by micro waving at 30% power for 2 to 2½ minutes. One 3-ounce package of cream cheese will soften in 1½ to 2 minutes.

Thaw frozen orange juice right in the container. Remove the top metal lid. Place the opened container in the microwave and heat on high power 30 seconds for 6 ounces and 45 seconds for 12 ounces.

Thaw whipped topping—a 4½ ounce carton will thaw in 1 minute on the defrost setting. Whipped topping should be slightly firm in the center but it will blend well when stirred. Do not over thaw!

Soften Jell-O that has set up too hard—perhaps you were to chill it until slightly thickened and forgot it. Heat on a low power setting for a very short time.

Heat hot packs in a microwave oven. A wet fingertip towel will take about 25 seconds. It depends on the temperature of the water used to wet the towel.

To scald milk, cook 1 cup for 2 to 2½ minutes, stirring once each minute.

To make dry bread crumbs, cut 6 slices into ½ inch cubes. Microwave in 3-quart casserole 6 to 7 minutes, or until dry, stirring after 3 minutes. Crush in blender.

Refresh stale potato chips, crackers or other snacks of such type by putting a plateful in the microwave oven for about 30 to 45 seconds. Let stand for 1 minute to crisp. Cereals can also be crisped.

Nuts will be easier to shell if you place 2 cups of nuts in a 1-quart casserole with 1 cup of water. Cook for 4 to 5 minutes and the nutmeats will slip out whole after cracking the shell.

For stamp collectors: place a few drops of water on stamp to be removed from envelope. Heat in the microwave for 20 seconds and the stamp will come right off.

Using a round dish instead of a square one eliminates overcooked corners in baking cakes.

A crusty coating of chopped walnuts surrounding many microwaved-cooked cakes and quick breads enhances the looks and eating quality. Sprinkle a layer of medium of finely chopped walnuts evenly onto the bottom and side of a ring pan or Bundt cake pan. Pour in batter and microwave as recipe directs.

Do not salt foods on the surface as it causes dehydration and toughens the food. Salt after you remove from the oven unless the recipe calls for using salt in the mixture.

Heat leftover custard and use it as frosting for a cake.

Melt marshmallow cream in the microwave oven. Half of a 7-ounce jar will melt in 35 to 40 seconds on high. Stir to blend.

Toast coconut in the microwave. Watch closely as it browns quickly once it begins to brown. Spread ½ cup coconut in a pie plate and cook for 3 to 4 minutes, stirring every 30 seconds after 2 minutes.

* * *

HERBS AND SPICES

Get acquainted with herbs and spices. add in small amounts, ¼ teaspoon for each 4 servings. Taste before adding more. Crush dried herbs or snip fresh herbs before using. If substituting fresh for dried, use 3 times more fresh herbs.

BASIL: Sweet warm flavor with an aromatic odor, used whole or ground. Good with lamb, fish, roast, stews, ground beef, vegetables, dressing and omelets.

BAY LEAVES: A pungent flavor, use whole leaf but remove before serving. Good in vegetable dishes, fish and seafood, stews and pickles.

CARAWAY: Has a spicy smell and aromatic taste. Use in cakes, breads, soups, cheese and sauerkraut.

CHIVES: Sweet mild flavor of onion, this herb is excellent in salads, fish, soups and potatoes.

CURRY POWDER: A number of spices combined to proper proportions to give a distinct flavor to such dishes as meat, poultry, fish and vegetables.

DILL: Both seeds and leaves of dill are flavorful. Leaves may be used as a garnish or cook with fish, soup, dressings, potatoes and beans. Leaves or the whole plant may be used to spice dill pickles.

FENNEL: Both seeds and leaves are used. Has a sweet hot flavor. Use in small quantities in pies and baked goods. Leaves can be boiled with fish.

GINGER: A pungent root, this aromatic spice is sold fresh, dried, or ground. Used in pickles, preserves, cakes, cookies, soups and meat dishes.

MARJORAM: May be used both dry or green. Used to flavor fish, poultry, omelets, lamb, stew, stuffing and tomato juice.

MINT: Leaves are aromatic with a cool flavor. Excellent in beverages, fish, cheese, lamb, soup, peas, carrots, and fruit desserts.

OREGANO: Strong aromatic odor, use whole or ground to spice tomato juice, fish, eggs, pizza, omelets, chili, stew, gravy, poultry and vegetables.

PAPRIKA: A bright red pepper, this spice is used in meat, vegetables and soups. Can be used as a garnish for potatoes, salads or eggs.

PARSLEY: Best when used fresh but can be used dry, use as garnish or seasoning. Try in fish, omelets, soups, meat, stuffing and mixed greens.

ROSEMARY: Very aromatic, used fresh or dried. Season fish, stuffing, beef, lamb, poultry, onions, eggs and bread.

SAFFRON: Orange yellow in color, this spice is used to flavor or color foods. Use in soups, chicken, rice and fancy breads.

SAGE: Use fresh or dried. The flowers are sometimes used in salads. May be used in tomato juice, fish, fondue, omelets, beef, poultry, stuffing, cheese spreads, cornbread and biscuits.

TARRAGON: Leaves have a pungent, hot taste. Use to flavor sauces, salads, meat, poultry, tomatoes and dressings.

* * *

VEGETABLE TIME TABLE

Vegetable	Cooking Method	Time
Asparagus tips	Boiled	10-15 min.
Artichokes, French	Boiled	40 min.
	Steamed	45-60 min.
Beans, Lima	Boiled	20-40 min.
	Steamed	60 min.
Beans, String	Boiled	15-35 min.
	Steamed	60 min.
Beets, young w/skin	Boiled	30 min.
	Steamed	60 min.
	Baked	70-90 min.
Beets, old	Boiled or Steamed	1-2 hours
Broccoli, flowerets	Boiled	5-10 min.
Broccoli, stems	Boiled	20-30 min.
Brussel Sprouts	Boiled	20-30 min.
Cabbage, chopped	Boiled	10-20 min.
	Steamed	25 min.
Cauliflower, stem-down	Boiled	20-30 min.
Cauliflower, flowerets	Boiled	8-10 min.
Carrots, cut across	Boiled	8-10 min.
	Steamed	40 min.
Corn, green, tender	Boiled	5-10 min.
	Steamed	15 min.
	Baked	20 min.
Corn on the cob	Boiled	8-10 min.
	Steamed	15 min.
Eggplant, whole	Boiled	30 min.
	Steamed	40 min.
	Baked	45 min.

Parsnips	Boiled	25-40 min.
	Steamed	60 min.
	Baked	60-75 min.
Peas, green	Boiled or Steamed	5-15 min.
Potatoes	Boiled	20-40 min.
	Steamed	60 min.
	Baked	45-60 min.
Pumpkin or Squash	Boiled	20-40 min.
	Steamed	45 min.
	Baked	60 min.
Tomatoes	Boiled	5-15 min.
Turnips	Boiled	25-40 min.

*   *   *

CONVERSION TABLE

MICROWAVE OVEN <—> CONVENTIONAL OVEN

For a 600 to 700 Watt Microwave Oven.
Settings by percentage: each 5% Microwave equals
22.5 degrees F in a Conventional Oven.

	Microwave	Percent	Conventional Setting
High	100		450 degrees
	95		427 degrees
	90		405 degrees
	85		382 degrees
Med. High	80		360 degrees
	75		337 degrees
	70		315 degrees
	65		292 degrees
Medium	60		270 degrees
	55		247 degrees
	50		225 degrees
	45		202 degrees
Med. Low	40		180 degrees
	35		157 degrees
	30		135 degrees
	25		112 degrees
Low	20		90 degrees
	15		67 degrees
	10		44 degrees
	5		23 degrees
	0		00 degrees

* * *

CONVERSION TABLE

MICROWAVE OVEN <—> CONVENTIONAL OVEN

For a 600 to 700 Watt Microwave Oven

Settings by Number

Microwave Number				Conventional Degrees
1	.	.	.	100 degrees
2	.	.	.	150 degrees
3	.	.	.	275 degrees
4	.	.	.	300 degrees
5	.	.	.	325 degrees
6	.	.	.	350 degrees
7	.	.	.	375 degrees
8	.	.	.	400 degrees
9	.	.	.	425 degrees
0	.	.	.	450 degrees

Some Microwave Ovens use a percentage setting while others use numbers 1 through 0 to indicate level of power being generated.

* * *

CALORIE COUNTER

BEVERAGES	Calories
Apple Juice, 6 ounces	90
Coffee, Black—unsweetened	0
Cola type, 12 ounces	115
Cranberry juice, 6 ounces	115
Ginger ale, 12 ounces	115
Grape juice, from frozen concentrate, 6 oz	142
Lemonade from frozen concentrate, 6 oz	85
Milk— Protein fortified, 1 cup	105
Skim, 1 cup	90
Whole, 1 cup	160
Orange Juice, 6 ounces	85
Pineapple juice, unsweetened, 6 ounces	95
Root beer non-diet, 12 ounces	150
Tonic, quinine water, 12 ounces	132

BREADS	
Corn bread, 1 small square	130
Dumplings, 1 medium	70
French toast, 1 slice	135
Muffins, bran, 1 muffin	106
Blueberry, 1 muffin	110
Corn, 1 muffin	125
English, 1 muffin	280
Melba Toast, 1 slice	25
Pancakes, 1 to 4 inch	60
Pumpernickel, 1 slice	75
Rye, 1 slice	60
Waffles, one	216
White, 1 slice	60 to 70
Whole wheat, 1 slice	55 to 65

CEREALS	CALORIES
Corn Flakes, 1 cup	105
Cream of wheat, 1 cup	120
Oatmeal, 1 cup	148
Rice Flakes, 1 cup	105
Shredded Wheat, 1 biscuit	100
Sugar Crisps, ¾ cup	110

CRACKERS	
Graham, 1 cracker	15-30
Rye Crisp, 1 cracker	35
Saltine, 1 cracker	17-20
Wheat Thins, 1 cracker	9

DAIRY PRODUCTS	
Butter or Margarine, 1 ounce	100
American Cheese, 1 ounce	100
Camembert, 1 ounce	85
Cheddar, 1 ounce	115
Cottage Cheese, 1 ounce	30
Mozzarella, 1 ounce	90
Parmesan Cheese, 1 ounce	130
Ricotta, 1 ounce	50
Roquefort, 1 ounce	105
Swiss, 1-ounce	105

CREAM CHEESE	
Light, 1 tablespoon	30
Heavy, 1 tablespoon	55
Sour, 1 tablespoon	45
Hot chocolate, with milk, 1 cup	277
Milk, chocolate, 1 ounce	145-155

YOGURT

made with whole milk, 1 cup	150-165
made with skimmed milk, 1 cup	125

EGGS

Fried, 1 large	100
Poached or boiled, 1 large	75-80
Scrambled or in an omelet, 1 large	110-130

FISH AND SEAFOOD

Bass, 4 ounces	105
Salmon, broiled or baked, 3 ounces	155
Sardines, canned in oil, 3 ounces	170
Trout, fried, 3½ oz	220
Tuna, in oil, 3 oz	170
Tuna, in water, 3 oz	110

FRUITS

Apple, 1 medium	80-100
Applesauce, sweetened, ½ ounce	90-115
Applesauce, unsweetened, ½ cup	50
Banana, 1 medium	85
Blueberries, ½ cup	45
Cantaloupe melon, ½ cup	24
Cherries, pitted, raw, ½ cup	40
Grapefruit, ½ medium	55
Grapes, ½ cup	35-55
Honeydew melon, ½ cup	55
Mango, 1 medium	90
Orange, 1 medium	65-75
Peach, 1 medium	35
Pear, 1 medium	60-100
Pineapple, fresh, ½ cup	40

Pineapple, canned in syrup, ½ cup   95
Plum, 1 medium   ..30
Strawberries, fresh, ½ cup   30

FRUITS

Strawberries, frozen and sweetened, ½ cup 120-140
Tangerine, 1 large   ..39
Watermelon, ½ cup   ..42

MEAT AND POULTRY

Beef, ground, lean, 3 oz   185
Beef, roast, 3 oz   185
Chicken, broiled, 3 oz   115
Lamb chop, lean, 3 oz   175-200
Sirloin steak, 3 oz   175
Tenderloin steak, 3 oz   174
Top round steak, 3 oz   162
Turkey, dark meat, 3 oz   175
Turkey, white meat, 3 oz   150
Veal cutlet, 3 oz   156
Veal, roast, 3 oz   176

NUTS

Almonds, 2 tablespoons   105
Cashews, 2 tablespoons   100
Peanuts, 2 tablespoons   105
Peanut butter, 1 tablespoon   95
Pecans, 2 tablespoons   95
Pistachios, 2 tablespoons   92
Walnuts, 2 tablespoons   80

PASTA

Macaroni or spaghetti, ¾ cup cooked   115

SALAD DRESSINGS

Blue cheese, 1 tablespoon	70
French, 1 tablespoon	65
Italian, 1 tablespoon	80
Mayonnaise, 1 tablespoon	100
Olive oil, 1 tablespoon	124
Russian, 1 tablespoon	70
Salad oil, 1 tablespoon	120

SOUPS

Bean, 1 cup	130-180
Beef, noodle, 1 cup	70
Bouillon and consommé, 1 cup	30
Chicken noodle, 1 cup	65
Chicken with rice, 1 cup	50
Minestrone, 1 cup	80-150
Split Pea, 1 cup	145-170
Tomato with milk, 1 cup	170
Vegetable, 1 cup	80-100

VEGETABLES

Asparagus, 1 cup	35
Broccoli, cooked, ½ cup	25
Cabbage, cooked, ½ cup	15-20
Carrots, cooked, ½ cup	25-30
Cauliflower, ½ cup	10-15
Corn, kernels, ½ cup	70
Green beans, 1 cup	30
Lettuce, shredded, ½ cup	5
Mushrooms, canned, ½ cup	20
Onions, cooked, ½ cup	30
Peas, green, cooked, ½ cup	60

POTATOES

baked, 1 medium	90
chips, 8 to 10	100
mashed, with milk and butter, 1 cup	200-300
Spinach, 1 cup	40
Tomato, raw, 1 medium	25
cooked, ½ cup	30

*   *   *

SOMETHING TO THINK ABOUT

I haven't thought about "fender skirts" in years. When I was a kid, I considered it such a funny term—made me think of a car in a dress.

Thinking about fender skirts, started me thinking about other words that quietly disappeared from our language with hardly a notice.

Like "Curb feelers" and "steering knobs". Since I'd been thinking of cars, my mind naturally went in that direction first, any kid will probably have to find some elderly person over 70 to explain some of these terms to you.

Remember "Continental kits"? They were rear bumper extenders and spare tire covers that were supposed to make any car as cool as a Lincoln Continental.

When did we quit calling them "Emergency brakes"? At some point "parking brake" became the proper term. But I miss the hint of drama that went with "Emergency Brakes".

I'm sad, too, that almost all of the old folks are now gone who would call the accelerator the "foot feed".

Didn't you ever wait at the street corner for your daddy to come home, so you could ride on the "running board" up to the house?

Here's a phrase I heard all of the time in my youth but never anymore: "store bought". Of course, just about everything is now store bought these days. But once it was bragging material to have a store-bought suit or a store bought bag of candy.

"Coast to coast" is a phrase that once held all sorts of excitement and now means almost nothing. Now we take the term "worldwide" for granted. This floors me.

On a smaller scale, "wall-to-wall" was once a magical term in most homes. In the 50's, everyone covered his or her hardwood floors with, wow, wall-to-wall carpeting!!! Today, everyone replaces their wall-to-wall carpeting with hard wood colors??? Go figure.

When was the last time you heard the quaint phrase "In a family way". It's hard to imagine that the word "pregnant" was once considered a little too graphic, or a little too clinical for use in polite company. So we had all that talk about stork visits and "being in a family way", or simply "expecting".

Apparently "brassiere" is a word no longer in usage. I said it the other day and my daughter cracked up. I guess it's just "bra" now. "Unmentionables" probably wouldn't be understood at all now.

It's hard to recall that this word was once said in a whisper, "divorce". And no one is called a "divorcee" anymore. Certainly not a "gay divorcee". Come to think of it," confirmed bachelors" and "career girls" are long gone too.

I always loved going to the "picture show", but I considered "movie" with affection.

Most of these words go back to the 50's, but here's a pure 60's word I came across the other day—"Rat Fink".
Ooh, what a nasty put down.

Here's a word I miss sometimes—"Percolator". That was just a fun word to say. And what was it replaced with? "Coffeemaker". How dull. Mr. Coffee, I blame you for this.

I miss those made-up marketing words that were meant to sound so modern and now sound so retro and old. Words like "Dynaflow" and "Electrolux. Or introducing the 1965 Admiral TV, now with "SpectraVision."

Food for thought. Was there a telethon that wiped out lumbago? Nobody complains of that anymore. Maybe that's what castor oil cured, because I never hear mothers threatening any of their kids with taking castor oil anymore.

Some words aren't gone, but are definitely on the endangered list. The one that grieves me the most is "supper". Now everybody says "dinner". Save a great word. Invite someone to supper, and discuss "fender skirts".

Someone forwarded this to me several years back when I first created my email address, and I thought that some of us that are of a certain age now (eighty plus) would remember most of these terms.

* * *

SOME HELPFUL HINTS YOU CAN USE AROUND YOUR HOUSE OR APARTMENT.

SEALED ENVELOPE—Put it in the freezer for a few hours, then slide a knife under the flap. The envelope can then be resealed.

Use empty toilet paper rolls to store appliance cords. It keeps them neat and you can write on the roll what appliance it belongs to.

For icy steps in freezing temperatures, get warm water and put Dawn dishwashing liquid in it. Pour it all over the steps. They won't refreeze. (I Wish I had known this forty years back.)

Crayon marks on walls?—This worked wonderfully. A damp rag, dipped in baking soda. Comes off with little effort (elbow grease, that is).

Permanent marker on appliances and counter tops; like store receipts that are usually blue; rubbing alcohol on a paper towel works fine.

Whenever I purchase a box of S. O. S. pads, I immediately take a pair of scissors and cut each pad into halves. After years of having to throw away rusted and unused and smelly pads, I finally decided that this would be much more economical. And now a box of these SOS pads last me indefinitely. In fact, I have noticed that my scissors get sharpened this way also.

Blood stains on clothes? Not to worry. Just pour a little hydrogen peroxide on a cloth and proceed to wipe off every drop of blood. Works every time. Now where to put the body?

Use vertical strokes when washing windows outside and horizontal stroke for inside windows. This way you can tell which side has the streaks. Straight Vinegar will get outside windows really clean. Don't wash windows on a sunny day. They will dry too quickly and will probably streak.

Spray a bit of perfume on a light bulb in any room to create a lovely light scent in each room when the light is turned on.

Place fabric softener sheets inside dresser drawers and your clothes will smell freshly washed for weeks to come. You can also do this with towels and linens too.

Candles will last a lot longer if they are placed in the freezer for at least three hours prior to burning.

To clean artificial flowers, pour some salt into a paper bag and add the flowers. Shake vigorously as the salt will absorb all of the dust and dirt and leave your artificial flowers looking like new!! Works like a charm....

To easily remove burnt on food from your skillet, simply add a drop or two of dish soap and enough water to cover the bottom of pan, and bring to a boil on stovetop.

Spray your Tupperware with nonstick cooking spray before pouring in tomato based sauces and there won't be any stains.

Wrap Celery in aluminum foil when putting in the refrigerator and it will keep for weeks.

When boiling corn on the cob, add a pinch of sugar to help bring out the corns natural sweetness.

Cure for headaches: Take a lime, cut it in half and rub it on your forehead. The throbbing will go away.

Don't throw out left over Wine. Freeze into ice cubes for future use in casseroles and sauces. Left over wine? What's that?

To get rid of itch from mosquito bites, try applying soap on the area and you will experience instant relief.

Ants, ants, ants everywhere. Well they are said to never cross a chalk line. So get your chalk out and draw a line on the floor or wherever ants tend to march. See for yourself!!!!

Use air-freshener to clean mirrors. It does a great job and better still, it leaves a lovely smell to the shine.

When you get a splinter in your finger or wherever, reach for the scotch tape before resorting to tweezers or a needle. Simply put the scotch tape over the splinter, then pull it off slowly. Scotch tape removes most splinters painlessly and easily.

Three tablespoons of reconstituted lemon juice equals the juice of one medium lemon.

*   *   *

WHAT YOU CAN DO WITH ALKA-SELTZER

Clean a Toilet. Drop in two Alka-Seltzer tablets, wait twenty minutes, brush and flush. The citric acid and effervescent action clean vitreous China.

Clean a vase. To remove a stain from the bottom of a glass vase or cruet, fill with water and drop in two Alka-Seltzer tablets.

Polish jewelry. Drop two Alka-Seltzer tablets into a glass of water and immerse the jewelry for two minutes.

Clean a thermos bottle. Fill the bottle with water, drop in four Alka-Seltzer tablets, and let soak for an hour or longer if necessary.

Unclog a Drain. Clear the sink drain by dropping three Alka-Seltzer tablets down the drain followed by a cup of Heinz white vinegar. Wait a few minutes, then flush with hot water.

* * *

SOME VERY OLD FASHIONED WAYS OF DOING THINGS

I liked the old paths, when Moms were at home. Dads were at work. Brothers went into the army. And sisters got married BEFORE having children....

Crime did not pay; Hard work did. And people knew the difference.

Moms could cook. Dads would work. Children would behave.

Husbands were Loving. Wives were supportive. And children were polite.

Women wore the jewelry. And men wore the pants. Women looked like ladies. Men looked like gentlemen. And children looked decent.

People loved the truth. And hated a lie. They came to church to get IN. Not to get OUT.

Hymns sounded Godly. Sermons sounded helpful. Rejoicing sounded normal. And crying sounded sincere.

Cursing was wicked. Drinking was evil. And divorce was unthinkable.

The flag was honored. America was beautiful. And God was welcome.

We read the Bible in public. Prayed in school. And preached from house to house. To be called an American was worth dying for. To be called a Christian was worth living for. To be called a traitor was a shame.

Sex was a personal word. Homosexual was an unheard of word, and abortion was an illegal word.

Preachers preached because they had a message. And Christians rejoiced because they had the VICTORY. Preachers preached from the Bible. Singers sang from the heart. And sinners turned to the Lord to be SAVED.

A new birth meant a new life. Salvation meant a changed life. Following Christ led to Eternal life.

Being a preacher meant you proclaimed the word of God. Being a deacon meant you would serve the Lord. Being a Christian meant you would live for Jesus. And being a sinner meant someone was praying for you.

Laws were based on the Bible. Homes read the Bible. And churches taught the Bible.

Preachers were more interested in new converts. Than new clothes and new cars. God was worshiped. Christ was exalted. And the Holy Spirit was respected.

Church was where you found Christians on the Lords day, rather than in the garden. Or on the creek bank, or on the Golf course, or being entertained somewhere else.

These old ways are still considered by me to be the best ways on most days.

*   *   *

PART THREE

CONTRIBUTORS' BRIEF BIOGRAPHIES

THE FOLLOWING ARE THE CONTRIBUTORS OF THESE
RECIPES IN THIS BOOK—— ALONG WITH A BIT OF
HISTORY ABOUT EACH OF THEM.

As part of their history there will be mentioned either a
wife or a husband along with some history about the second-
ary person.

{1} Alma Allora Emile Fehrs Corbin
    b) Mar 12 1900   d) May 24, 1974

Alma's real mother died soon after she gave birth to her second son {Herman} on April 25, 1901 at age 19 from complications following that birth.

Alma was raised by various family members until she started school. And since all of the members of her family were German, that meant that Alma spoke only German until she first went to school.

Alma attended a rural Cottonwood School, graduating in 1917. She clerked in a grocery store in Lily, South Dakota just prior to her marriage to Clarence Myron Corbin on November 26, 1919 after a proper courting period had passed.

Alma had eight children from 1922 to 1939. During the 1930's when most days consisted of blowing dirt from many miles away, like from the state of Kansas and Nebraska, This family kept themselves alive by farming what little they could grow in the family garden and because Alma was a great Seamstress, she made a little money by making dresses for other women of the other surrounding farms.

Even though money was not very prominent, because the Corbin family raised Chickens and Turkeys, wherefrom they got dozens of Eggs, which were used to barter with when buying whatever groceries they needed, and these two different kinds of fowl birds were also eaten when things got real scarce in the area of food.

This family raised Milk Cows where of the Milk of which they got from all of them, cream gleaned from that milk, and the excess milk was then fed to the Pigs that were used to sell and to butcher about twice a year. They also raised Sheep, which when was time for these sheep to be sheared, their wool that was a good way to make extra money also.

After both Alma and Clarence retired, they spent their

summers in South Dakota and their Winters in California visiting with all of their daughters. There was a son who lived in Southern California but they never visited with him ever. That son was Philip.

In 1969 they celebrated their 50th wedding anniversary in South Dakota and on March 27, 1972 Clarence died just thirteen days from being 85 years old.

Alma passed away on May 24, 1974 in Northridge Hospital after struggling with Colon Cancer for her last two years of her life. She was 74 years old. They both are buried at Prairie Hill Cemetery in Bradley, South Dakota.

* * *

{2} Catherin Adeline Nash Bosmoe
b) Jan 30, 1938   d) Oct. 14, 1976

Catherin Adeline Nash was born at the Bradley, South Dakota Hospital. She grew up on the family farm located 2 miles west and 2 miles south of Lily, South Dakota.

Catherin attended rural grade school near the farm at Cottonwood District #58 and she graduated from Bradley High School, Bradley, South Dakota in 1956.

Following graduation, the Northwestern Bell Telephone Company employed her for 19 years, working in its Webster, Sioux Falls and Aberdeen, South Dakota offices.

Catherin married Joseph Noel Bosmoe September 11, 1971 at Lily, South Dakota. Joe was born April 17, 1932 at Webster, South Dakota to the late Jacob Martin and Netty (Johnson) Bosmoe. He grew up on farms and attended rural grade school around Webster. His parents sent him to Fargo, North Dakota where he attended Oak Grove High School, graduating in 1950.

He then entered into the US Army in 1953, and took basic training at Camp Roberts, California and was subsequently sent overseas to Germany. Joe attended a radio operator school in Manheim, Germany and learned Morse code. After that training he worked as an Army radio operator. Due to illness and death of his father in May of 1954, Joe was given an honorable discharge from the Army after 18 months of service in order to return home and assume operation of the family farm—located 10 miles east of Pierpont, South Dakota.

Following their marriage Catherin and Joe operated the Bosmoe farm. Catherin suffered from Acute Leukemia for several years. She succumbed to that disease on October 14, 1976 at Rochester, Minnesota following a courageous struggle.

Catherin and Joe Bosmoe had two children and they are Christina Lou Bosmoe born November 13, 1972, and Sarah Jo Bosmoe born November 7, 1974.

Two years later, on November 18, 1978, Joe married Ruth Ann Elsing, who has four children, now grown from a previous marriage—surname Gallipo. Since then Joe and Ruth have had a son, Jacob William Bosmoe, who was born December 5, 1980 in Aberdeen, South Dakota. Joe is an active member of the American Legion and the Gideon Society. He continues to operate the family farm near Pierpont, and the family maintains a residence at 314 Avenue, NW, Aberdeen, South Dakota 57401-3342.

* * *

{3} Delores Arlene Storly Corbin
    b) Jul 23, 1932   d) Dec 24, 2011

Delores Arlene Storly was born in Webster, South Dakota to Joseph and Hulda (Thompson) Storly. The Storly's originally lived in Grenville, SD where Joseph managed the grain elevator there until his death in 1935. Hulda later remarried.

Delores graduated from Webster High School. Following graduation, she worked as an office clerk at Webster Produce Company, and was a cashier at the Webster Movie Theater until her marriage to Myron Henry Corbin in Colorado Springs, Colorado on February 10, 1951.

Myron was born October 11, 1927 on the family farm near Lily, South Dakota. Myron was killed on June 9, 1972 when a Dam north of Rapid City, SD, burst which caused a flood through that city and he was killed trying to help a woman and her seven children in a vehicle that was being swept away. This was the last time anyone had seen him alive on that fateful day. He was later found washed up onto a house roof as he lay out in the hot Sun. When his body was examined by a National Guard Doctor, it was determined that his body had been struck about waist high, with such a force that all of his blood ended up above his waist, therefore his upper body was all black. He was a white man.

His Casket was never opened so persons coming to his funeral could not see what he looked like when he died.

It was because Philip A Corbin requested it to be that way. And it was agreed to by the National Guard Doctors as well as the Commander of the unit that Myron was part of.

Myron attended school at Lily, SD from where he graduated from High school. He enlisted into the Marine Corp and served one year at El Toro Marine Base, in California. Myron had enlisted for a two-year term, but he opted to be discharged when the Corps adopted a new policy requiring the two-year enlistees to either commit for three years or be discharged. Myron decided to be discharged.

After being discharged from the Marine Corps, he took a job at a grain elevator near Omaha, Nebraska. But that did not work out well for him, so he returned to Lily and joined the South Dakota National Guard unit in Webster, SD. Myron's Guard unit was called into active duty when the Korean War was happening, and he served with the Unit on active duty in Colorado Springs and in Anchorage, Alaska.

Delores joined Myron while the unit was at the Colorado Springs Base and she went with him when he went to Alaska during his tour there.

Following the times with the National Guard, after the Korean War was over, Myron and Delores moved to a farm owned by Philip A Corbin, 1 ½ miles west of Lily, SD, working that farm until 1959, when he and Delores and family moved to Webster, SD and Myron took a job with the Milk Producers Association driving a Bulk milk truck.

Delores took a job as a grocery store cashier. Myron was also employed as a substitute mail carrier, and he managed the American Legion Club in Webster, SD.

At the time of his death, Myron was a First Sergeant of the 197th Field Artillery Battalion, SD National Guard, and was employed as a full time technician for the Webster, SD Unit.

Philip. Arden Corbin was personally involved in how the National Guard handled his body, and the Commander of his Unit asked me what should he do, because of what Myron's body looked like when it was found. I told him to not allow anyone who was personally involved with Myron to see his body, especially his wife, because I knew she would not want to remember how he looked at that time, but to have a Closed Casket at his funeral. And that is what happened. I personally did not attend his funeral, because my own wife was in a hospital in Irvine, California because she had had her first heart attack and I needed to be at home to take care of other obligations.

But I knew how his immediate family would react if they saw his body after that massive flood and where his body was found and in what condition it was found.

After Myron's death, Delores moved to Spearfish, SD where, for many years, she owned and operated two different motels. Delores also pursued many hobbies and she was an Avon Representative for her area. She resided at 223 Union Street, Spearfish, SD until her death.

Delores and Myron had four children and they are:

Vickie Lynn Corbin: b. Dec. 10, 1953
Craig Myron Corbin   b. Oct. 31, 1956
Rhonda Joy Corbin   b. Mar. 24, 1958
Cynthia Kay Corbin   b. Aug. 3, 1965

In 1980 when my sister Peggy and her husband Stanley Johnson, gave a party for myself, Philip A Corbin and my wife, Peggy Ann Corbin, on our 25th wedding Anniversary

At that time Delores Storly Corbin was visiting with my sister, and I took Delores aside and explained fully, without going into all of the gory details about why, at the funeral of Myron Corbin, his casket was kept closed, because of how he looked when Myron was found.

Delores told me that the National Guard Commander of the Unit that Myron was part of, told her basically the same thing, only using different words, and she knew that I was instrumental in making that decision along with his Unit Commander, and the Medical Examiner of the Army National Guard, but she thanked me anyway, because of how I described the situation, was more in line with how she always wanted to remember her husband and father of their children and how she would always remember him in her dreams.

*   *   *

{4} Jean Bruinier Transue Nash
b) Jun 10, 1930   d) Sep 23, 2012

I as the ultimate Author of this recipe book do not have much information about Jean Bruinier Transue Nash. But I know she has five children by a previous marriage a few years before 1948. And I will mention who they are in later paragraphs.

Jean Transue and Lee Nash were married on July 8, 1966 and it is likely that along with the three children that Lee had with his first wife Francis Ackley who were married December 11, 1949, that his three children and most of Jeans five children became one family after their marriage to each other. Whether Jeans five children were ever officially adopted by Lee is unknown to me.

So I will list each child as they have been reported to me previously from other writings, and they are:

Wendell Warren Nash, b. Aug 8, 1950

Dwight Nash, b. Aug 7, 1951

William Gilbert Nash, b. Apr. 7, 1960

Allan Lynard Transue, b. Oct 16, 1948

Devon Leslie Transue, b. Apr. 30, 1951

Ronald Dean Transue, b. Aug 17, 1954

Terry Lee Transue, b. Sep 27, 1958

Debbie Jean Transue b. Mar 17, 1962

Lee and Jean lived in Milwaukee, Oregon for many years where Lee worked in construction. They are now both retired and they reside at 600 East Saguaro Drive #181, Benson, AZ. 85602

* * *

{5} John Corbin Brice
   b) Aug 14, 1924   d) Nov 22, 2013

John attended Lily grade and high school, graduating in 1942. He moved, with his family, to Portland, Oregon on June 1, 1942.

He worked in the shipyards there until enlisting in the US Navy on July 3, 1943. John served 32 months in the Navy during World War II, being discharged in 1946, after the war was won in 1945.

Navy training consisted of boot Camp and Quartermaster School at Camp Farragut, Athol, Idaho. He served aboard the USS Algol, AKA 54 and saw some action in the Philippine Islands and Okinawa battle zones, earning 3 battle stars.

Following his discharge, he attended the University of Oregon, graduating in 1950 with a Bachelor of Arts degree in Education.

John served an additional 15 months with the US Navy during the Korean War, from July of 1950 to October of 1951. During that period, he served on the USS Paricutin, AE 18 an ammunitions ship operating in the waters off of Japan and Korea.

John married Blanche Mary Westover on October 25, 1952 in Richland, Washington. Blanche was born March 8, 1922 on a farm near Lily, SD. She was the daughter of Marie Sophia Sorensen and Charles Leslie Westover.

Marie was born November 16, 1899, in Chicago, Illinois and Charles was born December 22, 1889 on the family farm near Lily, SD. They were married November 17, 1920. Charles passed away on May 20, 1952, and Marie on September 2, 1991.

Blanche attended grade school through the 5th grade at East Cottonwood rural school in Clark County, SD. Her family then moved to Lily where she completed her education, graduating from High school in 1940.

She attended Northern State Teachers College, Aberdeen, SD, for one year and then taught for one year at a rural school west of Lily. Blanche then went to a Machinist school and worked in Logan and Provo, Utah.

She then joined the US Navy in May of 1943 and served until November of 1945. Naval training included Boot Camp at Hunter College, New York City, and Aviation Machinist School at Norman, Oklahoma. She also served at the Sandpoint Naval Air Station, Seattle, Washington, and Kaneohe Naval Air Station in Oahu, Hawaii. While at Sandpoint, Blanche was a superior marksman on the women's rifle team. From 1946 to 1948 she attended Business College in Seattle, WA, and was employed by General Electric in Richland, WA, from May 1948 to October 1952.

Blanche and John took up residence in Portland, Oregon in 1952. On February 29, 1952 John commenced 32 years and two months of employment with United Airlines. During most of this period with this Airline he was a Sales and Service Instructor.

He first worked in the Portland office, and then in 1975 he was transferred to Seattle, Washington, where he spent the remainder of his career, retiring May 1, 1984.

From March 1, 1985 to December 31, 1993, John performed 6,903 hours of volunteer service for the King County Police Department in Seattle, Washington. Blanche and John resided at 3015 NE 203rd Street, Seattle, WA. 98155.

They had four children and they are as follows:

Lee Duane Brice, b. August 19, 1953

David Lawrence Brice, b. February 27, 1955

Paul Charles Brice, b. August 16, 1956

Joan Clarice Brice, b. September 17, 1960

*   *   *

{6} Linda Ann Kirk Pierce
   b) Apr 12, 1957   d) May 1, 2011

Linda was born at Tyler, Minnesota to Francis and La-Donna {Leversedge} Kirk. Linda's family moved to Garvin, Minnesota before she started school. She attended Kindergarten to 6th grade at Balatop, MN. Then the family moved to Sacred Heart, MN where she attended high school.

Linda received her nurses training at Oklahoma City Community College, Oklahoma City, OK. She graduated as a registered nurse in 1989.

Linda married Leon Lyle Pierce September 17, 1977 at Sacred Heart, MN. Leon was born September 16, 1954 in Webster, South Dakota to Frank and Lyle {Corbin} Pierce. He grew up on the family farm southwest of Waubay, SD, He attended a rural grade school. Leon graduated from high school at Waubay in 1973.

At the end of 1996 Leon had completed 8 years as a truck driver. He first drove for Floyd Wild of Marshall, MN for almost 8 years. But in 1996 he began driving for Wynne Transport out of Omaha, Nebraska.

Prior to trucking, Leon worked on a road construction gang as a scraper operator, and worked several years for various farmers in South Dakota.

In 1984, Leon and Linda moved to Oklahoma when Leon worked at construction and Linda completed studies for her nursing degree.

Then Linda and Leon moved to Kansas in 1989, first to Newton, and then in 1991 to their present home in a Rural Route community in Valley Center, Kansas.

Linda has worked at the Halstead Hospital Cath Lab, Halstead, KS as a registered nurse for almost 7 years. She has also worked part-time in Home Healthcare.

Linda and Leon had three children and they are thusly:
Cassandra Ruth Pierce, b. August 24, 1976
Leah LaDonna Pierce, b. August 13, 1979
Jonathan Clayton Pierce, b. October 25, 1981

At the end of 1996 the two younger children, Leah and Jonathan were still attending high school and working part-time after school. Leah is a junior and works at a McDonald's fast food restaurant. She played flute and oboe in a Jazz band and high school band and she co-managed the wrestling team while in high school.

Jonathan is a 9th grader and worked at a local grocery store. Jonathan and Leon have spent the last two years at Motocross at that time. It was a hobby that both enjoyed at that time. Jonathan did the racing and Leon was the pit crew-mechanic.

In 1996 Jonathan broke his collarbone and missed the last part of the Motocross season, but even with all of that he placed 3rd place in the overall awards in his division. And he did receive a pretty good-sized trophy during the ceremonies at Ft. Worth, Texas in January of 1997.

* * *

{7} Lulu Elizabeth Corbin Nash
  b) Jan 20, 1896   d) Apr 3, 1988

Lulu attended grade school at York District #136 and graduated from high school in 1915. In fact 1915 was the first year any students graduated from the Lily, South Dakota High School.

Lulu secured teacher training at Aberdeen Normal College in Aberdeen, SD. and Spearfish Normal in Spearfish, SD. Lulu taught rural and town schools in Day, Beadle, and Meade Counties from 1917 to 1928.

As information Aberdeen Normal became Northern State Teachers College in Aberdeen, South Dakota.

She met and was courted by William Gilbert Nash and they eventually got married on December 24, 1927 in Aberdeen, SD.

In April of 1928, Lulu and Gil rented a farm located 2 miles west and 2 miles south of Lily, SD. They lived on that farm all of their lives, having purchased it in 1947. This farm still remains in the Nash family.

Times were especially hard during the "dirty thirties. Lulu told of having to light lamps in the middle of the day during dust storms. Gil worked with horse and wagon building roads for the Work Progress Administration {WPA} and told of driving his team of horses home during those dust storms. In fact he had to trust his team of horses because they always knew the way home.

Gil passed away in his sleep at the farm on February 7, 1958 at age 73 years, 4 months. Lulu continued to live on that farm helping her son, Gareld, who farmed the land.

In 1976 she retired and moved to Clark, SD. Much of her time in retirement was spent engaged in her favorite hobby, which was knitting clothes and making other things for all of the grandchildren and friends. She also helped her neighbors in any way she could. Both Lulu and Gilbert are buried in the Nash family plot at Prairie Hill Cemetery, Bradley, SD.

*   *   *

{8} Lyle Ramona Corbin Pierce
  b) Oct 23, 1917   d) May 15, 1992

Lyle Ramona Corbin Pierce was born on the family farm near Lily, South Dakota. She was baptized at the Lily Lutheran Church and later confirmed at Egeland Lutheran Church. She attended school in Lily.

She worked in Chicago, IL, and Watertown, SD before moving to the south Waubay, SD area. Lyle met and was courted by Frank Eugene Pierce and they were married on January 23, 1943 in Waubay. He was born on February 9, 1909.

The couple farmed south of Waubay for many years before retiring and moving into the town of Waubay in 1972.

Mr. Pierce died on April 5, 1974.

Lyle was employed as a school bus driver for the Waubay Public Schools from 1962 to 1984. She was instrumental in organizing the Waubay Senior Citizens Center, and was a member of Our Saviors Lutheran Church in Waubay. They had seven children.

*   *   *

{9} Margaret Ann Chapman Corbin
   b) Mar 23, 1930   d) May 27, 1996

Margaret grew up first in an old house in South St. Louis, Missouri until she was five years old. Then her parents were granted the opportunity to manage the Wabash Sports Club in Ferguson, Missouri, mostly because her Father {Lawrence Joseph Chapman} {Joe} worked for the Wabash Railroad as the Manager of the Mail and reproduction Department.

Whereof there was Kitchen capabilities at that Club and because there were always several families who always attended that Club every weekend, which was a way to make extra money for them and for the Club also. Because that Club had a lake on the grounds, where there was swimming allowed with Lifeguards and attendants who would help take care of all of the children who belonged to all of the members of this Club.

Because before you could come to this Club you had to be a member of it. There were fishing capabilities in this lake also. Including boats that members could rent. You see where this Club was located was an old Rock Quarry so this lake was very deep, so having qualified Lifeguards was mandatory, according to the City of Ferguson.

Margaret went to a Catholic girls School all the way through High School and that school was called St. Joseph's Academy, which was located in central south St Louis.

Margaret also attended St. Louis University in St Louis, Missouri and got an Associate of Arts degree in Pharmaceutical Science.

When Margaret had a position with a Company, which marketed, High School Year Books and she was the follow-up person who clinched the deal regarding these yearbooks. Because most small town schools and the senior class along with a chaperone would go to surrounding town's and sell advertisements that were placed at the end of each of these yearbooks. And because Philip Corbin was teaching several subjects at the Lily School, he became that chaperone.

So on September 28, 1955 at 1:20 pm Margaret met Philip Corbin and because he was also helping his father {Clarence Corbin} who was the Custodian of that school helping to sweep and clean every room in that school, Philip because he knew of the best towns to go to, to sell advertisements, Philip actually drove the vehicle {1955 Mercury Monterey} that Margaret was driving.

In fact Margaret about a week before this date, purchased this vehicle in Kansas City, Missouri, even though she did not have a driver's license on her person, nor had she made any payments on the vehicle.

After going to several towns within fifty miles of Lily, South Dakota the senior class and Philip Corbin sold enough advertising to more than pay for all of the High School Yearbooks for the year of 1955 and 1956.

In fact they had collected so much in advertising fees that the remainder of the money was saved so when the senior class graduated in the spring of 1956, this class could and did have themselves a private party, about June 1st of 1956.

So on Thursday September 29, 1955 when Margaret was preparing to go back to Webster, SD and her Hotel, Philip detained her long enough so he could talk to her, so these two persons sat in her vehicle near the garage at the Corbin residence and talked and necked and before this night ended, Philip convinced Margaret to stay the night at the Corbin residence, where Margaret was taken upstairs to his sister's bedroom, where Margaret got in bed with Philips sister {Betty}.

The next morning {Friday} when Philip brought Margaret downstairs, Mr. Klinger who was the Superintendent of the

Lily School at that time, was very surprised to see that she was still in the town of Lily and especially in the Corbin house. And so were Philip's parents surprised to see her in their house. So Margaret had a light breakfast and then Philip walked Margaret back to her vehicle, and then she drove away.

Philip was as nervous as a cat in a room full of rocking chairs for the rest of that day. But later that day when 5:00 PM came and then Margaret drove up the alley to where the garage is located, and Philip got into her vehicle on the driver's side and they drove away.

They first drove to Webster where Philip took a Wedding ring set to the Jewelry store where he had previously purchased it some months before, where he traded it for a different set of wedding rings plus a new wrist watch, of which he had never had before that day.

Then they headed east where Philip says he knows of a man in Ortonville, Minnesota who will marry us. It took about 2½ hours to get to Ortonville, where Philip drove to a particular building where Margaret and Philip got out of her vehicle. They walked into the building they had parked in front of, where a man who was obviously taller than Philip, he stood up and came and hugged Philip like he was a long lost son.

Philip introduced his lady friend as his future wife, whereof he expected this man to marry Margaret and himself soon. Anyway Judge Philip MacDonald told Philip that they have to buy a Wedding license before they can get married, and that man is now out of town, having gone to an Anniversary party of a longtime friend, and he will probably not be home until early the next morning, that being Saturday.

Usually the Courthouse is normally closed on Saturdays, but Judge MacDonald says he will order it to be opened just so you two can buy that wedding license. Then you two will come back to his office where he will marry us.

But for now I want you two to come to my house where you will be very welcome, because Judge MacDonald said he

does not know if Philip told you about me, but I am his Surrogate Father, meaning Philip lived with me and my wife and family for two years beginning in the fall of 1944 until about June of 1946.

The reasons are not important any longer, but this relationship was one that he will never forget. The Judge says he is very glad that Philip came to me because I always told him that if he ever needed me, he knew where to find me. The judge says you have grown into a handsome looking man. The Judge also says that my wife will be very glad to see you because we have talked about you many times.

Anyway when the next day arrived, we drove to where the Court House is located and because we were a bit early we waited for about a half hour before the Clerk of Courts showed up and he looked like he was death warmed over. He says he is still nursing a Hangover but he knows that you need him so you two can purchase a Wedding License.

He asked Margaret for some kind of identification and she says she does not have a driver's license. So Philip had to swear that she was actually 25 years old, even though at that time it was news to him, and of course Philip has a Driver's license so the license was issued. The entire costs of swearing that Margaret was 25 years old and the cost of the wedding license cost Philip eighteen dollars, which he says is well worth it.

Then we drove back to Judge MacDonald's office where he and Emma {his wife} and all of his offspring were waiting for us. We told Judge MacDonald that since we had first met at 1:20 PM on September 28 {three days previous} that we wanted him to announce us to be Husband and Wife at exactly 1:20 PM on this day, which is October 1, 1955. So that is how it happened.

Philip and Margaret were hugged many times that day, because they were not only hugged by Judge Philip MacDonald, but also by his wife Emma, and every one of his offspring and their husbands and or wives and children. Before we left Ortonville that family told us to come back every so often so they will know how we are doing. We exchanged addresses as to where they could write to us, and then we left and drove to Watertown, South Dakota, which was about a five-hour drive. They eventually went to St. Louis, Missouri, after Philip found a replacement teacher for himself.

Margaret and Philip remained in the St. Louis area for the next twelve and a half years, working in various fields.

Margaret worked at several different positions, but her main love was when working in the Accounting field, because she worked as a payroll Supervisor for many companies, both in the St Louis, Missouri area, Milwaukee, Wisconsin area and also in the Los Angeles, California area. After Philip worked for the Western Weighing and Inspection Bureau as a Traveling Auditor for 3 ½ years, he never took any of his vacation time during that time.

He decided he and Margaret would go to California for at least three months and because Philip did so many great things for this company, it was decided that Philip would get a total of four months' vacation fully paid for.

Margaret and Philip decided after being in California for two weeks, that they would remain in that state for how many years they would work there. And Margaret worked at various accounting positions in the Los Angeles area for about eight years and then she finally settled on working for the Union Oil Company as a Payroll Supervisor, handling all of the payrolls for all of the Ocean Oil Tankers that went to many different ports around this world. And one of the things she always like doing was having an Armored Truck pick her up where she worked, whereof it would go to whatever port several Oil Tankers were anchored, and with several thousand dollars, they would get on board of a motor launch and go to an Oil tanker and dispatch whatever moneys that were needed to pay to the crew of this ship, including the Captain of this Oil Tanker. Then they would go back to shore where these same guards would get several more thousand dollars from their Armored Truck and using the same motor launch would go to a different Oil Tanker and do the same as they did at the first tanker. But mostly they only went to one Oil Tanker.

In 1986 Margaret retired from the Union Oil Company and after remaining in Santa Ana, California for another four years she went with her Husband {Philip Corbin} who got himself a lateral transfer to Topeka, Kansas.

And then when Philip retired from the Atchison Topeka and Santa Fe Railroad, they moved to 1410 Stein Road in Ferguson, Missouri where Philip raised many different kinds of Flowers. Margaret died on May 27, 1996 after suffering from Stomach Cancer for many years. She is buried in Calvary Cemetery in St. Louis, Missouri.

* * *

{10} Neva Regina Martin Hazen Ruth
   b) Aug 4, 1916   d) Apr 1, 2002

Neva was born in Cavour, South Dakota and attended grade school there until age 10. Then the family moved to Seattle, Washington, where they lived for one year before moving to Boise, Idaho. In Boise, Neva attended St. Teresa's Academy for the rest of grade school and high school. She then attended Link's School of Business, and, following graduation, she found work in Pendleton, Oregon. It was in Pendleton that Neva met and became engaged to Leo Joseph Hazen. Because they were married on November 18, 1940, at Boise, Idaho with Neva's brother, Father Myron F. Martin conducting the ceremony.

Leo Hazen was born April 19, 1913 in Stanfield, Oregon. Leo joined the Merchant Marines during World War two. During that period Neva moved home to Boise and lived with her mother and father.

Neva's first child, Elizabeth, was born in Pendleton, Oregon, and the other children, Kathy, Marty, and Geri, were born in Boise, Idaho. Leo died October 2, 1966 in Portland, Oregon following Heart surgery.

Neva moved to Portland, Oregon in 1967 and found work with the Federal Government. It was in Portland that she met and was courted by Harold G. Ruth, and they were married February 12, 1972.

They retired and lived at Lincoln City on the Oregon Coast for seventeen years, then moved to the Woodburn, Oregon area to be closer to medical facilities.

Neva lost her beloved son, Marty in January of 1987, and she lost Harold on November 9, 1991.

After a year had gone by, Neva moved to her present location in a Summerfield apartment, which is an over 55 Senior Community. Apt. #12 in Tigard, Oregon 97224. She died there.

* * *

{11} Olive Elizabeth Brice Grace
    b) Oct 16, 1927   d) Dec 23, 1990

Olive was born in Lily, South Dakota to Leon and Vivian {Corbin} Brice. During her early years she lived in Lily where she attended school. The family moved to Portland, Oregon in June of 1942 where Olive attended a Girls Polytechnic high school, graduating in 1945.

Throughout high school, Olive did volunteer work as a Candy Striper at Emanuel Hospital in Portland. Following high school, she enrolled in Emanuel's school of nursing and in 1948 graduated as a registered nurse.

Olive then joined the US Army Nursing Corps and was assigned to Brooks Army Medical Center at San Antonio, Texas. She served as an Army nurse about one year before being discharged for the convenience of the government.

Olive met and was courted by William "Bill" Richard Grace, and they were married on June 30, 1949 at Stevenson, Washington. He was born March 4, 1927 in Portland, Oregon to Edward and Susan {Fehr} Grace. Edward was born in Lakeview, Oregon, and lived in Oregon all of his life. Susan was from Saskatoon, Saskatchewan, Canada. Both are now deceased.

Bill's early years were at Portland, OR. He enlisted in the US Navy in 1944 during World War Two and saw service as an aviation ordinance man on an aircraft carrier in the SE Asia Theater of operations.

He received an honorable discharge in 1946.

Bill is a 1947 graduate of Benson high school in Portland. He also holds a BS degree in political science from Portland State University awarded in 1987. Earlier in connection with his profession, Bill obtained an associate's degree in fire protection engineering.

Following Olive and Bill's marriage in 1949 the newlyweds took up residence in Portland where Bill had been employed since 1947 by the US Postal Service. He left that position in 1950 to take a job as a fireman with the Portland, Oregon Fire Bureau.

Over the ensuing years, Olive worked continually as a nurse at Emanuel Hospital except for the short periods of time off for the births of five children. Next to her family, her mission in life was delivering babies as a delivery room nurse. During the course of 40 years of her nursing career, Olive must have helped deliver over 5,000 babies. The many accolades from the new parents attested to her tender loving care of their newborn infants. While her own children were growing up, Olive would usually work the night shift at the hospital in order to be available for the children's daytime activities. Olive was the typical "sports mom" while her three sons were active in sports. In addition to attending all of their games of football, basketball and baseball, she often helped by keeping the teams records.

One year, for one of three son's leagues, she won a trophy as the league's best scorekeeper.

After her son Richard and his wife moved into a nearby home, Olive served as their baby sitter for many years,

Throughout her marriage Olive was active in local churches. During the last five years of her life she was an active member of the Mountain Park Baptist Church.

In 1982 Bill retired from the fire department after 33 years of service. Throughout the period of 1946 to 1987 Bill also served in various units of the US Naval Reserve, Army Reserve and Air National Guard. In 1987 he retired from the Air National Guard with a grade of Chief Master Sergeant.

It was about 1987 that Olive was diagnosed with Cancer. She succumbed to the disease on December 23, 1990.

* * *

{12} Roger Maurice Pitzl

b) May 18, 1944   d) Feb 16, 2005

Roger was born May 18, 1944 in Sleepy Eye, MN, the son of John Peter and Kathryn Mary Schwint Pitzl who were married June 5, 1937.

Roger grew up in the Hendricks, MN area. In 1960, at age 16, he enrolled in a 9-month course at Stevenson's Auto-Electric School in Kansas City, Missouri. After finishing that course, he went to Minneapolis, MN and found work as an auto mechanic.

Over the ensuing 46 years of consistent employment, up to the present date, Roger had acquired a broad range of skills through working in a wide variety of occupations. A sampling of his occupations include the following:

1962—factory work in St. Paul, MN making ice skates.

1964—service station operation in St. Paul, MN.

1966—factory work in Minneapolis making grease guns.

1969—moved to Redwood Falls, MN area and worked for Leonard Wittwere growing sugar beets on 500 acres.

1970—Jan-May—service station operation, Watertown, SD.

1970—grain elevator operation, Waubay, SD.

1971—road construction work in Wyoming.

1973—grain elevator construction in Evans, MN area.

1974—policeman for City of Waubay, SD.

1979-1988—truck driver, hauling grain for Joe Bisgard, driving a tanker truck for Jacobson Transport, and several other trucking jobs. One of his favorite CB handles was Captain Hook.

1989—auto repair shop owner-operator in Waubay, SD.

1994—small engine repair shop working out of his home.

1995—employed by City of Waubay in general maintenance.

Such a varied life as Roger's has seen its share of unusual incidents. Roger cites the following as most notable:

1959—Lost his left hand in a corn-picking machine.

1974/79—while a policeman, an altercation with a drunken Indian left Roger with a collapsed lung, requiring Emergency surgery.

1995—a ditch cave-in broke his pelvis in two places.

Roger is highly regarded in the area for his jack-of-all-trades skills. His main hobby is with the Buffalo Ridge Two-Cylinder Club, which is dedicated to the preservation and restoration of 2-cylinder John Deere tractors.

The family moved around quite a bit during the early years, mostly in Minnesota, Wyoming, and South Dakota.

But, in 1974 they settled in Waubay, SD where Roger and Verda built their own house. From 1969 to the late 1980s Verda was the homemaker. During recent years she has undertaken several outside jobs, and she is currently the Manager/Caretaker of The Waubay Housing Association, Inc., address is as follows:

Route 1, Box 9-H, Waubay, SD. 57273.

Roger and Verda had three children.

* * *

{13} Ruth Elaine Corbin Graves
  b) Jul 28, 1924   d) Mar 1, 2004

Ruth was born on the family farm to Clarence and Alma Corbin. She attended the Lily School, graduating from High School in 1942.

Following the graduation she traveled to California seeking employment, initially staying as a houseguest with Thelma and Charles Corbin in Modesto, California.

This was the early years of World War two, and jobs in the nation's defense plants were plentiful. For a time Ruth worked for a company that made crystals for radios, then she worked two years in a shipyard as a welder.

By the Wars ending in 1945 she had also worked as a clerk-typist for the U.S. Army. She was a telephone operator at the time of her marriage to Curtis Graves. Which was on May 2, 1947, and they lived in Ventura, California for more than fifteen years.

In 1962 they moved to a 160-acre farm in Polk County, Missouri near a town called Fairplay. Where they started a Dairy Farm operation. After eight years of milking many cows, they switched to an all beef cattle operation.

Then when things got a little tough Curtis went to work for the Frisco Railroad as a Piggyback loader, which means he had to back every trailer that came into that yard onto flatbed cars.

Curtis died on October 28, 1990 of complications due to cancer. In the town of Fairplay Ruth clerked for a while in a grocery store. And she died on March 1, 2004 of complications with her Type two Diabetes and Heart Disease.

*   *   *

{14} Vivian Irene Corbin Brice
    b) Mar 15, 1893   d) Jul 27, 1982

Vivian was raised on her parent's farmstead, near Lily, South Dakota. As a child Vivian saw Indian groups riding through their farm on horses.

Vivian went to grade school at a rural school, which was about a mile east and a quarter mile south of Lily. She went to High School in the town of Lily.

She told of being frightened by the big 18, 19, and 20-year-old boys who came in off the farms to go to school. These boys only went to school for a couple of months in the dead of winter and would rather fight than learn. These boys would have knock down fights with most of the teachers at the Lily School.

Vivian's younger sister Lulu was in the first formal graduating class from the Lily High School. There were no graduates before that year.

Vivian met Leon Druell Brice and they dated for a while until he returned to Lily after being discharged from the Army. He worked as a logger in northern Minnesota, and a sawmill worker in the Grays Harbor area of Washington State. He returned to South Dakota to enter into the Army where he served as an operating room orderly at Fort Bliss, Texas. After he was discharged from the army, he returned to Lily and married Vivian.

Vivian was one of the first telephone operators in the Lily telephone exchange. And she took in Teachers or students during the 1930 depression in order to make some extra money.

Vivian lived from the horse and buggy era to flying in Jet airplanes and men walking on the Moon. She is buried next to her husband in Willamette National Cemetery in Portland, Oregon.

* * *

{15} Esther Pauline Friedman aka Ann Landers
   b) Jul 4, 1918   d) Jun 22, 2002

Esther was born in Sioux City, Iowa. She has a sister whose name is Pauline Phillips, who is her twin sister.

Ann Landers took on that name because she wrote a Personal advice column and she was also an Author and a radio host. She went to High School in Sioux City until she graduated, then she went to Morningside College.

She married Julius Lederer and they were married from 1939 until 1975. They had one daughter whose name is Margo Lederer born in 1940. When Ann Landers died she lived in Chicago, Illinois at age 83.

*   *   *

{16} Philip Arden Corbin
aka P. Arden Corbin
aka P. A. Corbin
aka Doc Corbin
aka Dr. Phil Corbin
   b) Apr. 6, 1934   d)

You will note that this person has many names, mostly because he was throughout his years on this earth known as all of these names at one time or another. He was born on a farm in northeastern South Dakota where his father farmed 320 acres of land, using horses for most of that time.

Times might have been hard for some of his siblings, but for Philip they were sometimes very hard. An older brother by 31 months (Fritz) would always do something bad, but Fritz would tell his Dad that Phil did it, so Phil was the one who was always punished for not doing anything at all.

Anyway after Phil graduated from a different high school other than where he initially started his education in Lily, SD, he went to various Colleges in the US and eventually was awarded a Doctorate degree in Veterinary Medicine.

In 1977 he purchased an existing Veterinary Hospital, then three years later borrowed some money and expanded it to what it is today.

But Philip did not remain in California for more than another thirteen years, because he had many more experiences to fulfill before he was going to retire.

But does anyone ever retire, meaning to go home and become a couch potato?

This was not what Philip had in mind to do, because after he did retire he became known in the community where he lived in a town near St. Louis, Missouri as a person who was obviously well learned about how to grow many different kinds of flowers and especially Columnar Apple Trees of which in the year of 1995 was an experimental tree that had been developed by a Nursery in Clarksville, Missouri.

Then after his wife {Peggy} died on May 27, 1996 he worked at many different jobs in that area.

But after two more years went by he sold his house in that small town in northeastern St Louis County called {Ferguson, Missouri} and moved back to Topeka, Kansas where he met and married once again to a woman who had two sons from a previous marriage, and Philip and her {Barbara} got married on June 17, 2000.

But this marriage was not to last, because on April 4, 2007 his divorce was final, and that woman because she had other things on her mind, whereof those thoughts was another man from Colorado.

In 2005, Philip, after he had once again had another blackout, and after he came to consciousness, Barbara got him into a wheel chair and in trying to get him into her vehicle, Philip lost consciousness again and he was trapped between the wheelchair and her vehicle where he remained until the Paramedics arrived.

And it took three men to get him un-wedged from the position he was in. And because of that incident he lost the use of both of his legs for a long time. In fact he still has problems with both of his legs.

When Philip was ready to come home, Barbara instead had him placed in a Nursing Home, where she completely forgot about him because she did not come to see him very often. According to the Nursing Home records, she only came to see Philip four times while he was in that Nursing Home.

Besides when Philip was in that Nursing Home, he was being given drugs that took all of his conscious memories from him, because he now understands that his only living brother came to see him, and in fact that brother told of taking Philip on an outing for a while, but Philip does not have any memory of any of those happenings.

Isn't it amazing how Psychotropic Drugs can and do take any persons memories from that person. One day the Nurse that had been giving Philip all of those drugs, did not come to work and in fact she was gone for two whole days and nights. And during that time, Philip began to get his former memories back to his conscious memories, so when that Nurse did come back to work, Philip refused to allow any of those drugs to be injected into himself.

But a day later, that Nurse was fired from that Nursing home, and when she departed she took whatever records that existed for Philip Corbin dealing with those Psychotropic drugs and wherever she went to.

No one has ever heard from that Nurse since that time. This was in May of 2006.

For the next three months Philip did everything in his power to get himself out of that Nursing Home. Meaning he got appointments with every kind of doctor he figured would get him a clean bill of health, and on July 12th, 2006 Philip was discharged from that Nursing Home, and he vowed he would never return back to that Nursing Home. A year later that Nursing Home was permanently closed.

So once again Philip found himself Single again, and this time he told most of his few friends that he would never get married again. And he never did.

Then to wile away his time he began to write Books. He first wrote a Science Fiction Novel, then a Murder Mystery Novel, then an Historical Novel, then an Adventure Novel, then another adventure Novel, then a Novel about a lifetime of successes and failures, and then a Novel about Love, Hate, Success and Failure, Hurt and Forgiveness, and many more senses and experiences too numerous to mention here.

Philip now lives with two female Cats who literally watch over him as he does all that he does do. Philip is fighting a couple of different Cancers and different Cancers have plagued him since 2002. Some of these cancers are now in remission, but the one Cancer that has him worried is The Philadelphia chromosome-positive Chronic Myelogenous leukemia {Ph+CML}.

So he began taking a new drug called Bosulif on April 27, 2015. It has several side effects he has to watch out for and some of them can be fatal for him. Especially if he does not get himself to the Hospital in short order time.

It is sometimes said that the Cure is worse that the Disease. When Philip does eventually die, we all will miss this very talented man who affected so many persons lives with his general knowledge in so many different subjects and especially in the Veterinary Field of Medicines.

He never imposed himself on most person's lives except by all of the different articles that he wrote regarding so many different subjects.

Most persons did not really know him. They only got to know him by all of the stories that he would sometimes tell about himself and others. I personally will miss him a lot, because if it weren't for his knowledge about photography I would never have ever gotten my position with the company that I have worked for, for many years. Because when I wanted to quit going to College, he instead inspired me to take up Photography and Journalism and the rest is history.

Since 1969 I have called this man who loves animals like he has always loved me, and I call him Dad because he is a Dad to me.

My real father and Mother were killed in an automobile accident in South Dakota near the Black Hills area because he was heavily into Indian Politics.

And power does strange things to persons who end up being enemies to all of us who just wanted to live a normal life on an Indian Reservation, but Indian politics and White man's politics sometimes clash and persons often get hurt or killed, and that was where my real Father was in the mix of all of these clashes.

My real father was too powerful to continue living on this earth, so a contract to kill my Father was issued and late one night when I was visiting with a friend in another community, another automobile hit and ran my Father and Mother off of the road they were driving on, and over the side into a deep ditch, and they were supposedly killed instantly, according to the Highway patrol of South Dakota.

A friend of my Father who is also a friend of my Adoptive Dad contacted the Orphanage I had been put into, and next I was living in southern California in a large mansion that was more beautiful than I could have ever imagined. This friend of my new Dad always knew who needed help in South Dakota in the Indian Nations. And the rest of my life has been better than I could have ever imagined it would be.

On June 5, 2015 Philip was told that he no longer had to take any Cancer Drugs, at least for a little while, or until the cancer he was fighting came back on the scene for him.

Because the cancer drug called Bosulif is a dangerous drug because after it was taken for about a month, Philips kidneys began to deteriorate considerably.

So his Oncologist told him to stop taking it and after a week had gone by his kidneys were back to being close to normal. So this Oncologist says to not take this drug for another month and let's see how your body will respond and maybe you won't have to take any cancer drugs ever again. They did not tell Dad how his Cancer was faring, but Dad says he will inquire at a later date.

Thanks for keeping me totally informed about your life, Dad, as I have tried to do the same about my own life also. I hope and pray that you will live far beyond the age of one hundred years of age as I always like to hear you tell me about all of your many experiences that you have had in your life.

This is really a great Recipe Book. It's interesting that you have items in this book that I couldn't find anywhere else.

And thanks for asking me to write this little bit of history about you and me and all of the persons in your life.

If you had never came onto my scene back in 1969, I really don't know where I would have ended up at any juncture of my life.

Your Loving Son

John RB Corbin

*   *   *

THE END

Made in the USA
Middletown, DE
01 September 2024